INSTRUCTOR'S MANUAL TO ACCOMPANY
INTRODUCTORY ECONOMETRICS
WITH APPLICATIONS

Second Edition

RAMU RAMANATHAN
University of California, San Diego

THE DRYDEN PRESS
HARCOURT BRACE JOVANOVICH COLLEGE PUBLISHERS
Fort Worth   Philadelphia   San Diego   New York   Orlando   Austin   San Antonio
Toronto   Montreal   London   Sydney   Tokyo

ISBN: 0-15-546491-4

Printed in the United States of America

TABLE OF CONTENTS

INTRODUCTION

This instructor's manual consists of some remarks about the organization of the class, solutions to the remaining problems, and general guidelines regarding the use of the ECSLIB program. I would be grateful for comments about the text, "walk-through" applications, the ECSLIB program, manual, and practice sessions, as well as notification of typographical errors. They may be Faxed to (619) 534-7040 or sent to the following address.

Professor Ramu Ramanathan
Department of Economics
University of California, San Diego
La Jolla, CA 92093-0508, USA

Please feel free to call me at (619) 534-3383 with comments and suggestions.

ORGANIZATION OF THE COURSE

As mentioned earlier, Chapters 1 through 9 constitute the basic topics in econometrics that most instructors would want to cover. If students have taken a prior course on probability and statistics, then Chapter 2 can be skipped initially. You can refer students to this chapter, as needed, when the relevant concepts are used in later chapters. If there is no probability or statistics prerequisite for this course, then Chapter 2 can be covered in more detail. Students should try to work all the practice problems; they are usually short and the effort will be helpful in learning the subject matter better.

Chapters 10, 11, 12, and 13 are optional topics of a more advanced nature from which selections can be made as time permits. If the students are required to carry out an empirical project, it is recommended that Chapter 14 be assigned early.

Chapter 7 on the Lagrange multiplier (LM) test for model specification is likely to be new material, not usually covered in introductory courses. It is strongly recommended that this chapter be covered, even if only briefly, because the LM test is a powerful tool to aid in model specification, as will be seen from the examples in Chapter 7 and from its use in other chapters. It requires no more sophistication than the traditional Wald F-test.

PRACTICE COMPUTER SESSIONS WITH THE ECSLIB PROGRAM

As mentioned in the text, the ECSLIB program is easy to use, fast, and is designed to mesh coherently with the text. Students can, without much help from the instructor, carry out the practice sessions described at the end of each chapter and reproduce all the examples and "walk-through" applications. The program is currently available only for MS-DOS machines. However, source code (written in the C programming language) is available (at a cost of $500) to adopters for transporting to other machines (contact the author directly).

Initial checking of the program

The first step is to check and make sure that the diskette is not defective. If the diskette appears to be defective, then call the number (800) 447-9457 to get a replacement disk. A separate diskette that contains the ECSLIB commands for the empirical exercises in the book is available to instructors as a supplement to this instructor's manual and can be obtained by calling the number given above.

Documentations and Practice Sessions

Several executable programs and their documentation are included in the diskette accompanying the book. Appendix B has details about how to obtain the documentations and carry out practice computer sessions.

ANSWERS TO REMAINING PROBLEMS

CHAPTER 2

PRACTICE PROBLEMS

PP 2.1
$P(A) = P(A \cap T) + P(A \cap \bar{T}) = 0.03 + 0.07 = 0.1$. $P(\bar{T}) = 1 - P(T) = 1 - P(T \cap A) - P(T \cap \bar{A}) = 1 - 0.03 - 0.57 = 0.4$. $P(A \mid \bar{T}) = P(A \cap \bar{T})/P(\bar{T}) = 0.07/0.4 = 0.175$.

PP 2.2
Let F_1 be the event that the car selected by the first customer was a Ford and F_2 be the event that the car chosen by the second customer was a Ford. $P(F_2) = P(F_2 \cap F_1) + P(F_2 \cap \bar{F}_1)$, because the two events are mutually exclusive. The first term is $P(F_2 \mid F_1) P(F_1) = \dfrac{c+1}{c+d+1} \dfrac{a}{a+b}$. The second term is $P(F_2 \mid \bar{F}_1) P(\bar{F}_1) = \dfrac{c}{c+d+1} \dfrac{b}{a+b}$. Therefore, $P(F_2) = \dfrac{a(c+1) + bc}{(c+d+1)(a+b)}$.

PP 2.4
In the binomial example, we have $n = 20$, and $p = 0.25$. Therefore, $P(10 \text{ correct}) = \binom{20}{10} (0.25)^{10} (0.75)^{10}$.

PP 2.6
The expected win is $\left[5000 \times \dfrac{1}{10000} \right] + \left[2000 \times \dfrac{1}{10000} \right] + \left[500 \times \dfrac{1}{10000} \right] + \left[0 \times \dfrac{997}{10000} \right] = 0.75$.

PP 2.7
The average stock should be $(1 \times 0.1) + (2 \times 0.25) + (3 \times 0.3) + (4 \times 0.2) +$

$(5 \times 0.1) = 2.8$ dozens or 34 loaves of bread per day.

PP 2.8

(1) $P[Y|(X=0)] = P[Y \cap (X=0)]/P(X=0)$. For $Y=0$, this is $(16/36) \div (25/36) = 16/25$. Similarly, for $Y=1$, we have 8/25 and for $Y=2$, the conditional probability is 1/25. The procedure for the remaining parts is the same.

(2) The conditional probabilities that $Y = 0$, 1, or 2, when $X=2$ are, respectively, 1, 0, and 0.

(3) When $Y=0$, the conditional probabilities that $X = 0$, 1, or 2 are 16/25, 8/25, and 1/25.

(4) Given $Y=1$, the conditional probabilities for X are 8/10, 2/10, and 0.

(5) Given $Y=2$, the conditional probabilities for X are 1, 0, and 0.

PP 2.9

The calculations can all be done using the marginal densities of X and Y. We have $\mu_x = E(X) = \left[0 \times \dfrac{25}{36}\right] + \left[1 \times \dfrac{10}{36}\right] + \left[2 \times \dfrac{1}{36}\right] = 12/36$. It is easy to see that μ_y also has the same value. To obtain the variance, we first need $E(X^2)$ which is $\left[1^2 \times \dfrac{10}{36}\right] + \left[2^2 \times \dfrac{1}{36}\right] = 14/36$. Therefore, $\sigma_x^2 = E(X^2) - \mu_x^2$

$= \dfrac{14}{36} - \left[\dfrac{12}{36} \times \dfrac{12}{36}\right] = 10/36$. This is also equal to σ_y^2.

PP 2.10

$Cov(X, Y) = E(XY) - \mu_x \mu_y$. To obtain $E(XY)$ for Table 2.3, multiply the probability of each cell by the corresponding values of X and Y and sum over all the cells. The only nonzero entry is when $X = Y = 1$ with probability 2/36, so that $E(XY) = 2/36$. Therefore, $Cov(X, Y) = \dfrac{2}{36} - \left[\dfrac{12}{36} \times \dfrac{12}{36}\right] = -2/36$. From equation (2.7), the correlation coefficient is $-(2/36) \div (10/36) = -0.2$.

4

PP 2.12

The number of observations is 427 and hence $t^* = 1.96$. From the output for Practice Computer Session 2.4, for the high school GPA $\bar{x} = 3.56$ and $s = 0.42$. Therefore the required confidence interval for the average GPA is $3.56 \pm (0.42 / \sqrt{427}) \, 1.96 = (3.52, 3.60)$. The corresponding interval for college GPA is $2.79 \pm (0.54 / \sqrt{427}) \, 1.96 = (2.74, 2.84)$. For the confidence interval for the variance, we need the two 2.5 percent tails of the χ^2 distribution with 426 degrees of freedom. Using the ECSLIB program, it can be verified that $u_1 = 370.69$ and $u_2 = 485.05$. For the high school GPA, this gives the lower bound of the confidence interval for variance as $\dfrac{426(0.42)^2}{485.05} = 0.15$. The upper bound is $\dfrac{426(0.42)^2}{370.69} = 0.20$. The corresponding bounds for the variance of college GPA are $\dfrac{426(0.54)^2}{485.05} = 0.26$ and $\dfrac{426(0.54)^2}{370.69} = 0.34$.

EXERCISES

EX 2.1

Because A and B are independent, $P(A \cap B) = P(A) P(B)$. Therefore, $P(A) = P(B) = 0.6$.

EX 2.2

When a pair of dice is rolled, there are 36 possibilities each with a probability of 1/36. X can take values from 2 through 12. $X = 2$ can be represented by the point $(1, 1)$, where the first element is the outcome of the first die and the second element is the outcome of the second die. Hence $P(X = 2) = P(1, 1) = 1/36$. $P(X = 3) = P(1, 2) + P(2, 1) = 2/36$. By proceeding similarly, we obtain the frequency distribution of X as follows (this is known as a *triangular distribution*):

5

x	2	3	4	5	6	7	8	9	10	11	12
$f(x)$	$\dfrac{1}{36}$	$\dfrac{2}{36}$	$\dfrac{3}{36}$	$\dfrac{4}{36}$	$\dfrac{5}{36}$	$\dfrac{6}{36}$	$\dfrac{5}{36}$	$\dfrac{4}{36}$	$\dfrac{3}{36}$	$\dfrac{2}{36}$	$\dfrac{1}{36}$

EX 2.3
This is a binomial distribution with $n = 20$. Let X be the number of defective chips out of 20. We have $p = 0.1$. The computer will work if no more than 2 micro chips are defective. Thus, we need $P(X \leq 2) = P(X = 0) + P(X = 1) + P(X = 2)$. From Table A.6 we see that $P(X \leq 2) = 1 - P(X \geq 3) = 1 - 0.3231 = 0.6769$.

EX 2.5
Let X be the number of bulbs out of 20 ($= n$) that *do not* germinate. Then $p = 0.2$. My wife will not get a refund if $X \leq 2$. We therefore need $P(X \leq 2)$ for a binomial distribution with $n = 20$ and $p = 0.2$. From Table A.6, $P(X \leq 2) = 1 - P(X \geq 3) = 1 - 0.7939 = 0.2061$.

EX 2.7
$E(Z) = \Sigma_i (a + bx_i) f(x_i) = \Sigma_i a f(x_i) + \Sigma_i b x_i f(x_i) = a + b\mu_x$, because $\Sigma_i f(x_i) = 1$ and $\Sigma_i x_i f(x_i) = \mu_x$. By proceeding similarly, it is easy to verify that $E(Z^2) = a^2 + 2abE(X) + b^2 E(X^2)$. Therefore, $V(Z) = E(Z^2) - [E(Z)]^2 = a^2 + 2abE(X) + b^2 E(X^2) - (a + b\mu_x)^2 = b^2 [E(X^2) - \mu_x^2] = b^2 \sigma_x^2$.

EX 2.8
To obtain the mean of the triangular distribution given in the answer to Exercise 2.2, multiply each x by the corresponding probability and sum over all the entries. This gives the value 7 which could also have been obtained by noting that the distribution is symmetric around 7. To get $E(X^2)$, square each x first, then multiply it by the corresponding $f(x)$ and then sum over all x. We get $E(X^2) = 54.8333$. The variance and standard deviation are now 5.8333 and 2.4152 respectively.

EX 2.10

If the machine is rented for t hours, the revenue is $50t$, but it costs X^2 dollars because the machine breaks down periodically. The profit function is therefore $\pi(X, t) = 50t - X^2$. We are given that $E(X) = V(X) = 2t$. Hence expected profit is $E(\pi) = 50t - E(X^2) = 50t - [V(X) + \{E(X)\}^2] = 50t - 2t - 4t^2 = 48t - 4t^2$. From Appendix Section 2.A.2 we see that the condition for maximizing profits is $48 - 8t = 0$. Thus the optimum number of hours to rent is 6.

EX 2.12

(1) $P(A = 10)$ is obtained by summing the individual entries for $A = 10$, that is, $0.144 + 0.052 + 0.027 = 0.223$.

(2) $P(A = 10 \mid B = 3) = P(A = 10, B = 3)/P(B = 3) = 0.027 \div (0.027 + 0.066 + 0.098) = 0.1414$.

(3) $E[B \mid (A = 20)] = \dfrac{(1 \times 0.126) + (2 \times 0.118) + (3 \times 0.066)}{0.126 + 0.118 + 0.066} = 1.8065$.

(4) $E(B) = 1 \times (0.144 + 0.126 + 0.063 + 0.024) + 2 \times (0.052 + 0.118 + 0.097 + 0.057) + 3 \times (0.027 + 0.066 + 0.128 + 0.098) = 1.962$.

$P(A=10, B=1) = 0.144$, $P(A=10) = 0.223$, and $P(B=1) = 0.357$. It is readily seen that $P(A=10, B=1) \neq P(A=10)\, P(B=1)$. Therefore the events are not statistically independent.

EX 2.13

2.5a $Var(aX + bY) = E[(aX + bY)^2] - [E(aX + bY)]^2$. The first term is $E(a^2X^2) + E(b^2Y^2) + E(2abXY) = a^2E(X^2) + b^2E(Y^2) + 2abE(XY)$. The second term is $a^2[E(X)]^2 + b^2[E(Y)]^2 + 2abE(X)E(Y)$. Grouping terms appropriately, we have $Var(aX + bY) = a^2 [E(X^2) - \{E(X)\}^2] + b^2 [E(Y^2) - \{E(Y)\}^2] + 2ab[E(XY) - \{E(X)E(Y)\}] = a^2Var(X) + b^2Var(Y) + 2abCov(X, Y)$. The special case follows by setting $a = 1$ and $b = \pm 1$.

2.5c Let $f(x, y)$ be the joint density of X and Y, and μ_x and μ_y be the corresponding means. $Cov(X, Y) = E(XY) - \mu_x\mu_y$. Because of independence, $f(x, y) = f(x)f(y)$. Hence $E(XY) = \Sigma_{xy}xy\, f(x) f(y)$. But x and y are separable in the summation and hence we have

$$E(XY) = [\Sigma_x \, xf(x)] \, [\Sigma_y \, f(y)] = E(X)E(Y)$$

It follows therefore that the covariance is zero. Because the correlation coefficient has the covariance as the numerator, it is also zero. In this case, the covariance terms in 2.5a drop out.

2.5e $Cov(X, X) = E(X^2) - [E(X)]^2 = Var(X)$. It follows from this that the correlation coefficient between X and itself is 1.

2.5f   To prove this we need only a counter example. Let $U = X + Y$ and $V = X - Y$, where X and Y have each mean zero, the same variance σ^2, and covariance $\sigma_{xy} \, (\neq 0)$. Then $E(U) = E(V) = 0$ and $Cov(U, V) = E(UV) = E(X^2 - Y^2) = 0$. Thus U and V are uncorrelated even though X and Y have the correlation coefficient σ_{xy}/σ^2.

EX 2.15

Each x_i has expectation μ and hence $E(\Sigma x_i) = n\mu$. It follows that $E(\bar{x}) = \mu$. From Property 2.A.1c, $Var(\Sigma x_i) = n\sigma^2$ because the x_i's are independent and identically distributed. Hence $Var(\bar{x}) = \sigma^2/n$. $E(y) = \dfrac{1}{n}\Sigma a_i \mu = \mu \dfrac{1}{n}\Sigma a_i$. For this to be equal to μ, the condition is $\Sigma a_i = n$. Also, $V(y) = \dfrac{\sigma^2}{n^2}\Sigma a_i^2$.

EX 2.16

We have, $n = 81$, $\bar{x} = 739.98$ and $s = 312.7$. From the t-table, $t^*_{80}(0.025) = 1.993$ (interpolating between 60 and 120 d.f.). The confidence interval for the mean claim is therefore, $739.98 \pm [(312.7/9)\,1.993] = (670.734, \, 809.226)$. Because this confidence interval includes the value 800, we accept the null hypothesis that the population mean is 800. The assumption needed is that the sample claims be a random sample from the same distribution.

EX 2.18

The test statistic is $F_c = [(n-2)r^2]/[1-r^2]$, where $n = 26$ and $r = 0.37$. Under the null hypothesis of zero correlation, the test statistic has an F-distribution with 1 d.f. for the numerator and 24 d.f. for the denominator. From Table A.4a we note that $F^*_{1,24} = 7.82$. Also, $F_c = 3.807$ which is less than F^* and hence we cannot rejected the null hypothesis.

EX 2.20

(1) The mean value of the houses is $\bar{y}$ = 107226/500 = 214.452 thousands of dollars. The mean income is $\bar{x}$ = 24838/500 = 49.676. The sample variances are given by equation (2.11). The values are 66398/499 = 133.062 for income and 1398308/499 = 2802.22 for house value. The standard deviations are the corresponding square roots, namely, 11.535 and 52.936.

(2) The correlation between the two variables is given by equation (2.13). We have

$$r_{xy} = \frac{194293}{(66398)^{\frac{1}{2}} (1398308)^{\frac{1}{2}}} = 0.638.$$

(3) Assuming that the sample houses are drawn independently from the same population, the confidence interval for the mean value of houses is $\bar{y} \pm [(s_y/\sqrt{n})t^*_{499}]$ = 214.452 $\pm$ [(52.936/$\sqrt{499}$) 1.96] = 214.452 $\pm$ 4.645 = (209.807, 219.097).

(4) The test statistic is $F_c = [(n-2)r^2]/[1-r^2]$, where n = 500 and r = 0.638. Under the null hypothesis of zero correlation, the test statistic has an F-distribution with 1 d.f. for the numerator and 498 d.f. for the denominator. From Table A.4a we note that $F^*_{1,498}$ = 6.63. Also, F_c = 341.9 which is greater than F^* and hence we reject the null hypothesis and conclude that there is a significant correlation between household income and the value of houses.

CHAPTER 3

PRACTICE PROBLEMS

PP 3.4

The required relationship is $F = \alpha + \beta W + u$, where F is fuel consumption per mile and W is the weight. Time series data would be for a single ship over time. But the weight of the ship is usually the same for all time periods. When discussing Assumption 3.3 (Section 3.1) we have seen that the model cannot be estimated if all the observations on the independent variable are the same. This problem does not arise with cross-section data. Ships will differ in the values for F and W and hence the model can be estimated.

PP 3.8

The null and alternative hypotheses are, H_0: $\beta = 0.1$ and H_1: $\beta \neq 0.1$. The computed t-statistic is $t_c = (0.13875-0.1)/0.01873 = 2.069$. Under the null hypothesis, this has a student's t-distribution with 12 degrees of freedom. The critical values of t are 2.179 and 3.055 for 5 percent and 1 percent levels of significance respectively. Because the absolute value of t_c is less than these critical values, we accept the null hypothesis that $\beta = 0.1$.

PP 3.10

For a one-tailed test (H_0: $\beta = 0$, H_1: $\beta > 0$), the coefficient is insignificant at the 10 percent level if $t_c < t_{12}^*(0.1)$, where t^* is the point on the t-distribution such that the area to the right is 0.1. For a lower significance level (say 5 percent), $t_{12}^*(0.05)$ must be greater than $t_{12}^*(0.1)$. Hence t_c must be less than $t_{12}^*(0.05)$ also, implying that the coefficient is insignificant at the 5 percent level. It is readily seen that this argument applies to any level below 10 percent.

PP 3.12

The original model is $\widehat{PRICE} = \hat{\alpha} + \hat{\beta}$ SQFT. Substituting $1000 + X^*$ for SQFT, we have, $\widehat{PRICE} = \hat{\alpha} + \hat{\beta}(1000 + X^*) = \hat{\alpha} + 1000\hat{\beta} + \hat{\beta}X^* = \hat{a} + \hat{b}X^*$. Therefore, $\hat{a} = \hat{\alpha} + 1000\hat{\beta}$ and $\hat{b} = \hat{\beta}$.

PP 3.14

The data file *DATA3-14* and the following ECSLIB commands will be useful in obtaining the necessary information to answer the question.

```
ols gnp 0 pop;
fcast 1989 1989 f1
genr time
ols gnp 0 time;
fcast 1989 1989 f2
summary time pop ;
smpl 1989 1989
print f1 f2 -o ;
```

For 1989 the actual value of GNP is 4117.7. The forecast from the first model is 3809.9 and the corresponding confidence interval is (3491.8, 4128.0). For the second model, the values are 3862.7 and (3621.1, 4104.3). Neither model has predicted GNP accurately but the second model with a time trend has smaller forecast error and a narrower confidence interval (note that equation 3.27 is used to compute the forecast variance).

PP 3.15

From Example 3.A.2, the elasticity is $\beta X/Y$ for the linear model and from Example 3.A.3 it is β/Y for the linear-log model.

PP 3.16

The slope is given by $\Delta Y/\Delta X = \beta/X$ which is negative. Also, the absolute value of the slope becomes smaller and smaller as X increases. if $\alpha = 0$, the graph will be as drawn below. For positive values of α the curve will shift upwards.

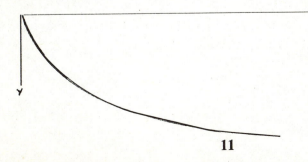

PP 3.18

If β is negative, then Y increases as X increases. Also the absolute value of the slope becomes smaller as X increases. The graph will therefore be as follows.

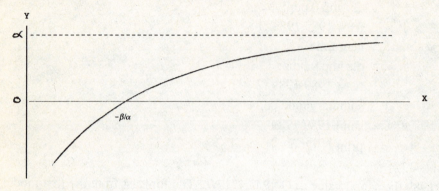

PP 3.19

The test statistic is $t_c = (1 - 0.82977)/0.09438 = 1.804$. From the t-table we note that for 12 d.f. t_c is larger than t^* at 5 percent but smaller than that at 2.5 percent (one-tail test). The actual pvalue is 0.048.

EXERCISES

EX 3.2

The scatter diagram for this is given below.

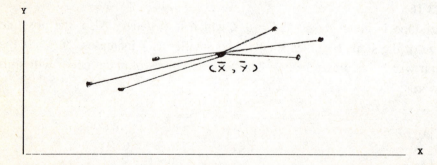

The estimate of the slope is now

$$\hat{\beta} = \frac{1}{T} \Sigma \left[\frac{Y_t - \bar{Y}}{X_t - \bar{X}} \right]$$

To compute the expected value note that $Y_t - \bar{Y} = \beta(X_t - \bar{X}) + u_t - \bar{u}$. As before, the error terms have expectation zero and hence $E(Y_t - \bar{Y}) = \beta(X_t - \bar{X})$. It readily follows that $\hat{\beta}$ is unbiased. By the Gauss-Markov Theorem, this is inferior to the OLS estimator.

EX 3.3

(a) The term $(Y_t - Y_{t-1})/(X_t - X_{t-1})$ is the slope of the straight line connecting the adjacent points (X_{t-1}, Y_{t-1}) and (X_t, Y_t). Therefore, $\tilde{\beta}$ is the average of the slopes of the straight lines connecting successive data points.

(b) We have,

$$\frac{Y_t - Y_{t-1}}{X_t - X_{t-1}} = \frac{\alpha + \beta X_t + u_t - \alpha - \beta X_{t-1} - u_{t-1}}{X_t - X_{t-1}} = \beta + \frac{u_t - u_{t-1}}{X_t - X_{t-1}}$$

Hence,

$$\tilde{\beta} = \beta + \frac{1}{T-1} \sum_2^T \left[\frac{u_t - u_{t-1}}{X_t - X_{t-1}} \right]$$

X_t is nonrandom and $E(u_t) = E(u_{t-1}) = 0$. Therefore, $E(\tilde{\beta}) = \beta$, which means that $\tilde{\beta}$ is unbiased. By the law of large numbers, $\frac{1}{T-1} \sum_2^T u_t$ converges to its expectation, which is zero. It follows that $\tilde{\beta}$ converges to β as $T \to \infty$. Thus, $\tilde{\beta}$ is consistent. Here also we need the assumptions that X_t is nonrandom and that $E(u_t) = 0$ for all t.

13

(c) By the Gauss-Markhov Theorem, OLS estimates are most efficient among unbiased linear estimators. This implies that any other such estimator, in particular $\tilde{\beta}$, is inefficient (or at least is no more efficient) than the OLS estimate.

EX 3.5

The model is $Y_t = \beta X_t + u_t$.

(a) The slope of the straight line from the origin to (X_t, Y_t) is Y_t/X_t. The average of this for $t = 1, 2, \cdots T$ is $\beta^* = \dfrac{1}{T} \Sigma \left[\dfrac{Y_t}{X_t} \right]$.

(b) $\dfrac{Y_t}{X_t} = \dfrac{\beta X_t + u_t}{X_t} = \beta + \left[\dfrac{u_t}{X_t} \right]$

As before, X_t is nonrandom and $E(u_t) = 0$. Hence $E(Y_t/X_t) = \beta$ and $E(\beta^*) = \beta$. β^* is thus unbiased.

(c) By the Gauss-Markhov Theorem, OLS estimator is the most efficient (has the smallest variance among unbiased linear estimators), and hence is superior to β^*.

EX 3.6

The estimated coefficient is $\hat{\beta} = \Sigma X_t Y_t / \Sigma (X_t^2)$. Substitute from the true model to obtain

$$\hat{\beta} = \frac{\Sigma[X_t(\alpha + \beta X_t + u_t)]}{\Sigma X_t^2} = \alpha \frac{\Sigma X_t}{\Sigma X_t^2} + \beta + \frac{\Sigma X_t u_t}{\Sigma X_t^2}$$

The expected value of the third term is zero because $E(u_t) = 0$. But $\hat{\beta}$ will be biased unless the first term is also zero. The required condition is therefore that $\Sigma X_t = 0$ or that the sample mean is zero.

EX 3.7
$Cov(X_t, \hat{u}_t) = E(X_t\hat{u}_t) - X_tE(\hat{u}_t)$. Note that X_t is non-random and $\hat{u}_t$ is a linear combination of the u's with zero expectation. It follows that the covariance between X_t and $\hat{u}_t$ is zero.

EX 3.10
The proof of this is in the derivation of equation (3.7´).

EX 3.11
From equation (3.7), $\hat{\beta} = S_{xy}/S_{xx}$, where S_{xx} and S_{xy} are defined as in equations (3.8) and (3.9). Also, from equations (2.11) and (2.12), $S_{xx} = (T-1)s_x^2$ and $S_{xy} = (T-1)s_{xy}$. $\hat{\beta}$ can be rewritten as follows:

$$\hat{\beta} = \frac{S_{xy}}{S_{xx}} = \frac{S_{xy}}{s_x^2} = \frac{S_{xy}}{s_x s_y} \cdot \frac{s_y}{s_x} = r\frac{s_y}{s_x}$$

because $r = s_{xy}/(s_x s_y)$ from equation (2.13).

EX 3.13
The regression model will have the form $S_t = \alpha + \beta t + u_t$, where t is time from 1 through 25. The data column for the dependent variable will be just the sales in each of the years and that for t will take the value 1 for the first year, 2 for the second year, and so on. The estimated sales in the 28th year is $\hat{\alpha} + 28\hat{\beta}$.

EX 3.14
To answer this question, examine the expression for R^2 given in equation (3.23) and ask yourself what happens when Y is a constant for all observations.

EX 3.15
The normal equation for this model is given by $\Sigma X_t\hat{u}_t = \Sigma X_t(Y_t - \hat{\beta}X_t) = 0$. The sum of squares ΣY_t^2 can be written as

$$\Sigma Y_t^2 = \Sigma(Y_t - \hat{Y}_t + \hat{Y}_t)^2 = \Sigma(\hat{u}_t + \hat{Y}_t)^2 = \Sigma\hat{u}_t^2 + \Sigma\hat{Y}_t^2 + 2\Sigma\hat{u}_t\hat{Y}_t$$

The third term is zero because

$$\Sigma \hat{u}_t \hat{Y}_t = \Sigma \hat{u}_t \hat{\beta} X_t = \hat{\beta} \Sigma X_t \hat{u}_t = 0$$

by the normal equation just stated. It follows from this that $\Sigma Y_t^2 = \Sigma \hat{Y}_t^2 + \Sigma \hat{u}_t^2$.

EX 3.17

The elasticity of Y with respect to X is $\eta = \dfrac{X}{Y} \dfrac{\Delta Y}{\Delta X}$. For the elasticity to be constant, η must be independent of X and Y. The appropriate model is the double-log model $\ln Y = \alpha + \beta \ln X + u$, discussed in Section 3.13 (see also Example 3.A.1 of Appendix 3.A). To estimate this model, first generate new variables, say $Y2 = \ln Y$ and $X2 = \ln X$. Then regress $Y2$ against a constant term and $X2$. The coefficient for $X2$ is the estimated elasticity of Y with respect to X.

EX 3.18

(a) In Section 3.6 we described how to test the model as a whole with an F-test. The null hypothesis is that X and Y are uncorrelated (that is $\rho_{XY} = 0$) and the alternative is that they are correlated. The test statistic is $F_c = R^2(T-2)/(1-R^2)$. In our example, $T = 427$ and the F-statistics for the three models are, respectively, 84, 32, and 60. For a 1 percent-level of significance, the critical $F_{1,425}^*(0.01)$ is approximately 6.7. Because the calculated F-values are well above this, we reject the null hypothesis of lack of correlation between X and Y and conclude that they are correlated. This means that all three models are significant overall.

(b) The null hypothesis is that a particular regression coefficient is zero. The alternative for a two-tailed test is that it is nonzero. The critical $t_{425}^*(0.0025)$ is slightly above 2.807. If an observed t-value exceeds this (in absolute terms) we reject the null hypothesis and conclude that the coefficient is statistically significant. The calculated t-values are:

16

$$0.92058/0.20463 = 4.50$$
$$0.52417/0.05712 = 9.18$$
$$1.99740/0.14128 = 14.14$$
$$0.00157/0.00028 = 5.61$$
$$1.62845/0.15135 = 10.76$$
$$0.00204/0.00026 = 7.85$$

Because all the *t*-statistics exceed the critical value, every regression coefficient in every model is statistically significantly different from zero.

(c) The low values for R^2 indicate that the independent variables HSGPA, VSAT, and MSAT do not explain much of the variance in COLGPA. We will see in later chapters that a more extended model does better.

EX 3.20

  (a)

$$\widehat{cost} = -796.075 + 53.451 \; miles$$
$$\quad\quad\;\; (-5.9) \quad\;\; (18.3)$$

$$R^2 = 0.858 \quad\quad\quad d.f. = 55$$

$$\widehat{cost} = -626.240 + 7.349 \; weeks$$
$$\quad\quad\;\; (-6.0) \quad\;\; (22.2)$$

$$R^2 = 0.899 \quad\quad\quad d.f. = 55$$

  (b) As *miles* or *weeks* increase, we would expect the cost to increase also. The slope coefficients would therefore be expected to be positive, which they are. When *weeks* or *miles* are zero, we would expect cost to be zero also. The constant terms would be expected to be zero. The actual signs are negative and counterintuitive. This indicates possible model misspecification. For instance, suppose the actual relation between Y and X is curvilinear as in the following figure and starts at the origin. But if we fit a straight line to the data, the estimated intercept term might be negative. This example suggests that the sign and magnitude of the estimated constant term might be unimportant.

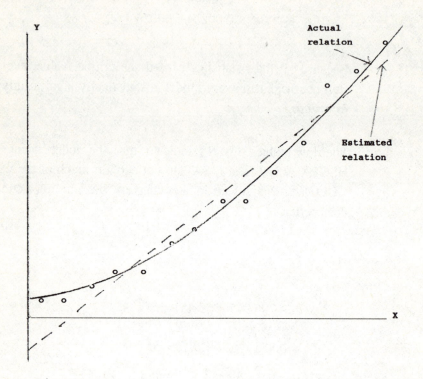

(c)   The t-statistics for both $\hat{\alpha}$ and $\hat{\beta}$ are very high and indicate significance. The critical t^{*} for 55 d.f. is about 3.5 for the 0.1 percent level. Both t-values are well above this which means that the regression coefficients are statistically very significantly different from zero.

(d)   The second model fits better because it has a higher value for R^2. Thus the age of the car is a better predictor than the mileage. However, since the gain in R^2 is only 0.041, the improvement in fit is not much.

18

(e)   If *miles** is the actual miles, then *miles** = 1000 *miles*. The estimated first model is *cost* = - 796.075 + 0.053451 *miles**. Only the coefficient for *miles** and its standard error are affected. R^2, *t*-, and *F*-statistics are unchanged.

EX 3.21

The estimated model is given below:

VARIABLE	COEFFICIENT	STDERROR	T STAT	PROB t > |T|
0) constant	16.10100	1.70015	9.470	< 0.0001 ***
2) assets	1.69657e-04	7.02050e-04	0.242	0.8111
Unadjusted R-squared	0.002			
F-statistic (1, 24)	0.058	Prob. F > 0.058 is 0.811097		

The degrees of freedom are 24 and the critical value for 10 percent (two-tailed) is $t^*_{24}(0.05) = 1.711$. We note that the regression coefficient for assets has a *t*-statistic below this, indicating insignificance. This is confirmed by the *p*-value which is 0.8111. Because there is a 81.11 percent chance of making a Type I error, we cannot reject the hypothesis that the regression coefficient for assets is zero. The overall significance is tested by the *F*-test. The test statistic is 0.058 with the same *p*-value as above and hence the model as a whole does not explain the variation in returns to capital (as indicated by R^2, only 0.2 percent is explained). This result is not too surprising because food processing is a competitive industry and there are no serious barriers to entry. Thus, if a particular company has "excess" returns, then free entry would attract new companies and this would push the returns back to "normal". The results indicate that there are no economies to the scale of operation. Rates of return would depend on other factors such as the the wage rate, interest rate, cost of materials and other inputs.

EX 3.22
The scatter diagram and estimated model given below indicate a good fit.

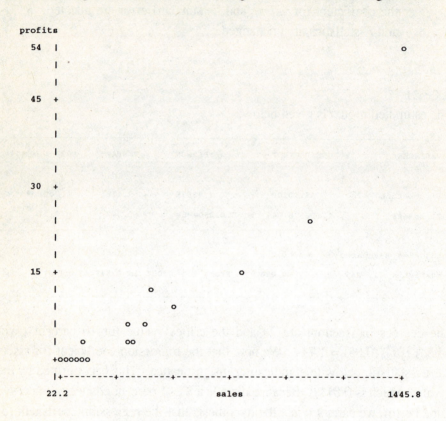

VARIABLE	COEFFICIENT	STDERROR	T STAT	PROB t > |T|
0) constant	-0.73282	0.71033	-1.032	0.3105
2) sales	0.02968	0.00181	16.423	< 0.0001 ***
Error Sum of Sq (ESS)	328.64322	Std Err of Resid. (sgmahat)		3.30980
Unadjusted R-squared	0.900	Adjusted R-squared		0.897
F-statistic (1, 30)	269.730	Prob. F > 269.730 is < 0.00001		

The standard error of residuals and the standard errors of individual coefficients are presented in the above table, as are the t-statistics and the corresponding p-values. The constant term is significant only at the 31 percent level but the coefficient for sales is extremely significant with a p-value below 0.01 percent.

Let PROFIT* be profits in millions of dollars. Then PROFITS = PROFITS* /1000. Substituting this in the model, we get PROFIT* = - 732.82 + 29.68 SALES. Thus both regression coefficients are multiplied by 1000. The standard errors will also be multiplied by 1000 and the error sum of squared will be multiplied by a million. However, R^2, t-, and F-statistics are independent of units and will be unchanged.

EX 3.23
The estimated coefficients and associated statistics are given below.

VARIABLE	COEFFICIENT	STDERROR	T STAT	PROB t > |T|
0) constant	41.58369	5.20811	7.984	< 0.0001 ***
1) years	1.60429	0.30200	5.312	< 0.0001 ***

Unadjusted R-squared	0.530		
F-statistic (1, 25)	28.220	Prob. F > 28.220 = 0.000017	

The scatter diagram presented in the next page does not indicate a good fit.

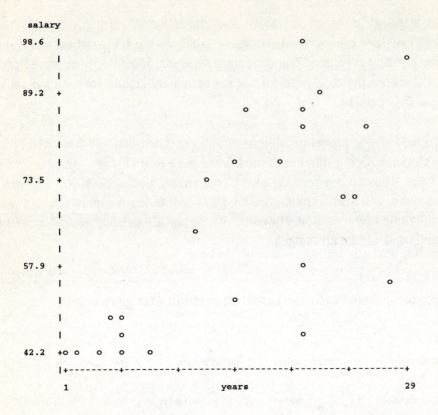

```
  salary
    98.6  |                                                      o
          |                                                                o
          |
    89.2  +                                               o
          |                               o               o
          |                                               o              o
          |
          |                           o           o
    73.5  +                    o                                    o  o
          |
          |
          |               o
          |
    57.9  +                                               o
          |                                                              o
          |                           o
          |          o  o
          |             o                                 o
    42.2  +o  o     o        o        o
          |+---------+---------+---------+---------+---------+---------+
            1                          years                         29
```

The test for overall significance is given by the *F*-statistic in the above table. Because it has an extremely low *p*-value, we conclude that the correlation between salary and number of years since Ph.D. is significantly different from zero. The *p*-values for both the constant and the coefficient for years are below 0.0001 indicating significance at levels below 0.01 percent. However, the model explains only 53 percent of the variation in salaries and is hence inadequate. Number of years since Ph.D. is not the only variable that would influence salaries. A Professor's publication record, reputation among peers, visibility in the profession, and so on, are very important and hence measures of these characteristics should be included in the model.

22

EX 3.24

The scatter diagram and estimated model given below indicate a poor fit.

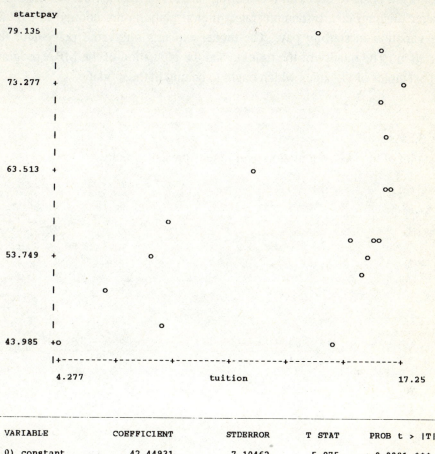

VARIABLE	COEFFICIENT	STDERROR	T STAT	PROB t > |T|
0) constant	42.44931	7.10462	5.975	< 0.0001 ***
1) tuition	1.26610	0.49931	2.536	0.0207 **
Unadjusted R-squared	0.263			
F-statistic (1, 18)	6.430	Prob. F > 6.430 = 0.020709		

The *F*-statistic is significant at the level 0.020709. *p*-values for the constant term and the coefficient for tuition are very small indicating that tuition has a significant positive effect on the starting salaries of MBA's. However, as the scatter diagram clearly demonstrates, tuition alone is not enough to explain the variation in starting pay. The model explains only 26.3 percent of the variation. The quality of the training and the reputation of the MBA program are examples of variables which ought to belong in the model.

EX 3.25

The plot of the U.K. population over time is presented below.

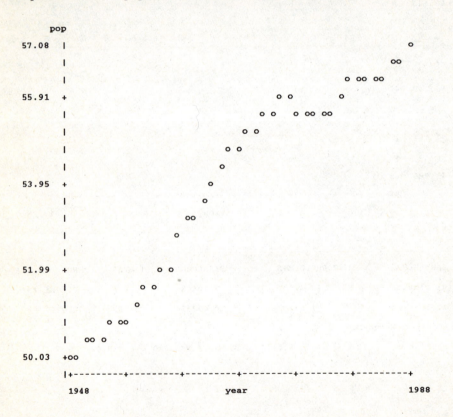

Estimated time trend and associated statistics are presented below.

VARIABLE	COEFFICIENT	STDERROR	T STAT	PROB t > |T|
0) constant	50.23028	0.18487	271.701	< 0.0001 ***
3) time	0.18519	0.00767	24.145	< 0.0001 ***
Unadjusted R-squared	0.937			
F-statistic (1, 39)	582.992	Prob. F > 582.992 = < 0.00001		

From the graph we see that a linear trend is not quite appropriate. A polynomial relation might be better. However, the value of R^2 is 0.937 indicating that time explains 93.7 percent of the variation in U.K. population. The p-value for the F-statistic is extremely small and hence the overall fit is quite good. Both the intercept and slope terms are significant at levels below 0.01 percent. Population has been growing at an average annual rate of 0.18519 millions.

EX 3.26

In contrast to the U.K model, the time trend tracks U.S. population well, as shown in the plot on the next page. The estimated coefficients are presented below along with associated summary statistics.

VARIABLE	COEFFICIENT	STDERROR	T STAT	PROB t > |T|
0) constant	147.31778	0.52888	278.545	< 0.0001 ***
3) time	2.44965	0.02094	116.991	< 0.0001 ***
Unadjusted R-squared	0.997			
F-statistic (1, 41)	13687.003	Prob. F > 13687.003 = < 0.00001		

Time explains 99.7 of the variation in U.S. population. The p-values for each of the regression coefficients and for the F-statistic are very low and hence the model fits the data extremely well. On average, U.S. population has been growing at the rate of 2.44965 millions.

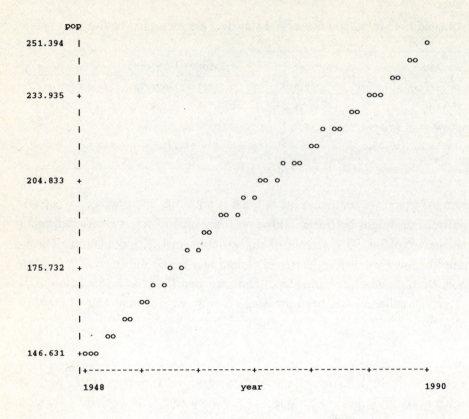

```
     pop
 251.394  |                                                              o
          |                                                        oo
          |                                                     oo
 233.935  +                                               ooo
          |                                            oo
          |                                      o  oo
          |                                    oo
          |                                 o  oo
 204.833  +                              oo  o
          |                            o  o
          |                         oo  o
          |                       oo
          |                     o  o
 175.732  +                  o  o
          |                o  o
          |              oo
          |            oo
          |      -  oo
 146.631  +ooo
          |+---------+---------+---------+---------+---------+---------+
            1948                       year                      1990
```

EX 3.27

The estimated Engel Curve is presented below and the graph is on the next page.

VARIABLE	COEFFICIENT	STDERROR	T STAT	PROB t > |T|
0) constant	0.41556	0.42232	0.984	0.3300
2) income	0.06743	0.00367	18.380	< 0.0001 ***

Unadjusted R-squared	0.873	
F-statistic (1, 49)	337.836	Prob. F > 337.836 = < 0.00001

The simple linear regression model explains 87.3 percent of the variation in the expenditure on travel, which is quite good for a cross section study. The overall goodness of fit test has an *F*-statistic of 337.836 which is extremely significant. The intercept term has a *p*-value of 0.33 which means that it is not significant even at the 25 percent level. The slope term, however, is highly significant. An increase of one billion dollar in income is expected to increase the average expenditure on travel by 0.06743 billions of dollars or by 67.43 millions of dollars. The graph, however, shows several points away from a regression line. This suggests that there are some missing variables. The size of the population of a state might be an important determinant of the expenditures. Also important are factors such as whether the state has milder weather patterns (as in California and Florida) or not and whether adequate air travel facilities are available in the state. Winter travel is quite difficult in the Northern States and would affect total expenditures.

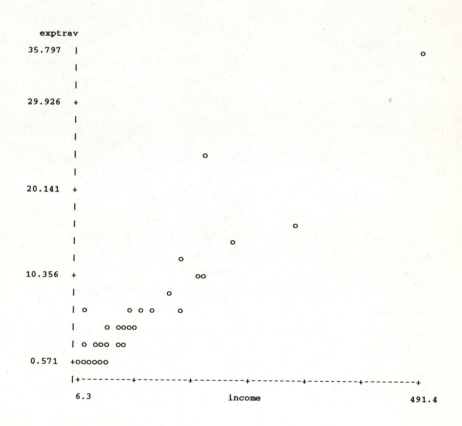

EX 3.28

The graph of GNP against the population and the corresponding regression output are presented below.

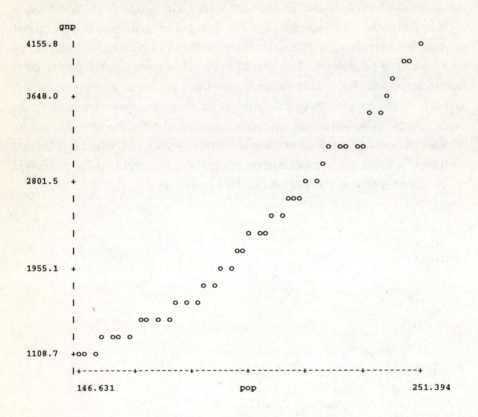

VARIABLE	COEFFICIENT	STDERROR	T STAT	PROB t > |T|
0) constant	-3380.49286	159.17789	-21.237	< 0.0001 ***
3) pop	28.90464	0.78220	36.953	< 0.0001 ***
Unadjusted R-squared	0.971			
F-statistic (1, 41)	1365.525	Prob. F > 1365.525 = < 0.00001		

The graph indicates a possible good fit except for a few years. R^2 is 0.971 which is extremely significant with a very high F-statistic. Both the intercept and slope terms are significant at levels below 0.01 percent. If population increases by one million, then GNP is expected to increase, on average, by 28.90464 billion dollars.

The estimated coefficients and associated statistics for a model in which a time trend is fitted are presented below.

VARIABLE	COEFFICIENT	STDERROR	T STAT	PROB t > |T|
0) constant	865.41728	36.75011	23.549	< 0.0001 ***
4) time	71.36338	1.45495	49.049	< 0.0001 ***
Unadjusted R-squared	0.983			
F-statistic (1, 41)	2405.770	Prob. F > 2405.770 = < 0.00001		

The time trend model explains a larger fraction of the variation in GNP (R^2 is 0.983). On average, GNP increase at the rate of 71.36338 billions of dollars.

EX 3.29
Taking the logarithm of the sales relation, we have the log-linear model $\ln S_t = \ln S_0 + t \ln(1 + g) + u_t$. Hence $\ln S_0 = 3.6889$ and $\ln(1 + \hat{g}) = 0.0583$. Therefore, $\hat{S}_0 = e^{3.6889} = 40.000822$, and $\hat{g} = e^{0.0583} - 1 = 0.060033$. Hence, the annual average growth $\hat{g}$ is approximately 6 percent. Five years into the future, $\hat{S}_{t+5} = S_t(1 + \hat{g})^5 = 1.3384 S_t$.

EX 3.30
The graph of the quantity of sealing compound against its price given in the next page indicates a very poor simple linear relation. Clearly there are other determinants of the quantity demanded such as the amounts of different types of construction activities.

29

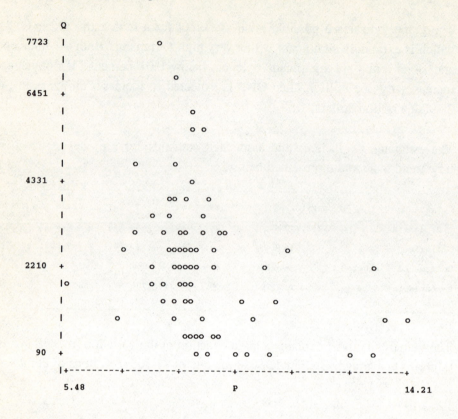

```
        Q
7723  |                  o
      |
      |                o
6451  +
      |              o
      |             o  o
      |
      |        o    o
4331  +             o
      |          oo o    o
      |        o  o     o
      |     o    o oo  o  oo
      |   o     oooooo  o            o
2210  +        o   ooooo  o        o            o
      |o        o o  ooo
      |          o o oo      o    o
      |   o        o   o        o          o   o
      |          oooo oo
  90  +            o o   o o   o        o   o
      |+---------+---------+---------+---------+---------+---------+
        5.48                        P                      14.21
```

The estimated simple linear model is presented below.

VARIABLE	COEFFICIENT	STDERROR	T STAT	PROB t > |T|
0) constant	5962.05375	955.80996	6.238	< 0.0001 ***
3) P	-381.09238	104.76573	-3.638	0.0005 ***
Unadjusted R-squared	0.132			
F-statistic (1, 87)	13.232	Prob. F > 13.232 = 0.000466		

The conclusion from the graph is reinforced by the low R^2 value. However, it is still statistically significantly different from zero because the F-statistic has a p-value below 0.0005. The null hypothesis here is that the correlation between quantity and price is zero and the alternative is that it is not zero.

The test statistic F_c has the F-distribution with d.f. 1 for the numerator and 87 for the denominator. The test criterion is to reject the null hypothesis if the p-value is below the level of significance. Price has the expected negative sign and the coefficient is significantly different from zero at the 0.0005 level. Here the test statistic is the ratio of the coefficient divided by its standard error. Under the null hypothesis that the regression coefficient is zero, the test statistic has the t-distribution with 87 d.f. An increase of one dollar in price is expected to decrease, on average, the demand for the sealant by 381 gallons per month.

The estimated double-log model has the following coefficients and associated statistics.

VARIABLE	COEFFICIENT	STDERROR	T STAT	PROB t > |T|
0) constant	12.99814	1.18220	10.995	< 0.0001 ***
5) ln(price)	-2.47997	0.53965	-4.596	< 0.0001 ***
Unadjusted R-squared	0.195			
F-statistic (1, 87)	21.119	Prob. F > 21.119 = 0.000015		

Here also the overall goodness of fit is highly significant, as are the individual regression coefficients. The price elasticity of demand is - 2.47997 which means than a one percent increase in the price will reduce demand by 2.47997 percent. To test whether the elasticity is unitary or not (only the absolute value matters for this test), the test statistic is $t_c = (|\hat{\beta}| - 1)/s_{\hat{\beta}} = (2.47997 - 1)/0.53965 = 2.742$. It is readily verified that this is significant at the 1 percent level. Hence we reject the unitary elasticity hypothesis. Because the estimated elasticity is numerically larger than 1 we conclude that demand is elastic.

CHAPTER 4

PRACTICE PROBLEMS

PP 4.1

The change in expected average price is given by

$$\widehat{\Delta PRICE} = \hat{\beta}_2 \, \Delta SQFT + \hat{\beta}_3 \, \Delta BEDRMS + \hat{\beta}_4 \, \Delta BATHS$$

$$= (0.1548 \times 350) - 21.588 - 12.193 = 20.399$$

The increase in price is thus \$20,399, which appears reasonable.

PP 4.2

The forecast (in thousands of dollars) is $129.062 + (0.1548 \times 2500) - (21.588 \times 4) - (12.193 \times 3) = 393.131$, which appears reasonable.

PP 4.4

The model is $Y_t = \alpha + \beta X_t + u_t$. From Property 4.2, $\hat{\beta}^* = \hat{\beta} s_x / s_y$. But $\hat{\beta} = Cov(X, Y)/Var(X) = Cov(X, Y)/s_x^2$. Substituting this, $\hat{\beta}^* = Cov(X,Y) / (s_x \, s_y)$, which is the same as the simple correlation coefficient between X and Y.

PP 4.5

$$\bar{R}^2 = 1 - \frac{ESS(T-1)}{TSS(T-k)} = 1 - \frac{\hat{\sigma}^2(T-1)}{TSS}$$

We readily see that $\bar{R}^2$ and $\hat{\sigma}^2$ move inversely to each other.

PP 4.9

See Practice Computer Session 4.1.

PP 4.10

The *F*-statistic with Model C as the unrestricted model and Model D as the restricted model is given by

$$F_c = \frac{(ESS_D - ESS_C)/3}{ESS_C/10} = \frac{(101815 - 16700)/3}{1670}$$

which is 16.989, the same value reported in Table 4.2 for Model C. The calculations for Models A and B are similar. For Model D, the error sum of squares (ESS) is $\Sigma(Y_t - \hat{\beta}_1)^2 = \Sigma(Y_t - \bar{Y})^2$, which is the same as the total sum of squares (TSS). Therefore $R^2 = 1 - (ESS/TSS) = 0$. It is easy to see that $\bar{R}^2$ is also zero.

PP 4.11

Solving the first restriction for β_3, we have $\beta_3 = 1 - \beta_2$. Substituting this in equation (4.5), we get $Y_t = \beta_1 + \beta_2 X_{t2} + (1 - \beta_2)X_{t3} + u_t = \beta_1 + X_{t3} + \beta_2(X_{t2} - X_{t3}) + u_t$. Bringing the X_{t3} term, which has no regression coefficient, to the left we obtain the restricted model as

$$Y_t - X_{t3} = \beta_1 + \beta_2(X_{t2} - X_{t3}) + u_t$$

From the second restriction, we have $\beta_3 = -\beta_2$. Substituting this in the unrestricted model and regrouping terms, we get the restricted model

$$Y_t = \beta_1 + \beta_2(X_{t2} - X_{t3}) + u_t$$

PP 4.13

The Cobb-Douglas production function gives rise to the double-log model

$$\ln Q_t = \beta_1 + \alpha \ln K_t + \beta \ln L_t + u_t$$

Substituting $\beta = 1 - \alpha$ in this we get,

$$\ln Q_t = \beta_1 + \alpha \ln K_t + (1-\alpha) \ln L_t + u_t$$
$$= \beta_1 + \ln L_t + \alpha(\ln K_t - \ln L_t) + u_t$$

Bringing $\ln L_t$ (which has no unknown coefficient) to the left-hand side,

$$\ln Q_t - \ln L_t = \beta_1 + \alpha(\ln K_t - \ln L_t) + u_t$$

The procedure is to generate two new variables; $Y_t = \ln Q_t - \ln L_t$ and $X_t = \ln K_t - \ln L_t$. Then regress Y_t against a constant and X_t. $\hat{\beta}$ is obtained as $1-\hat{\alpha}$.

PP 4.14

Taking logarithms of both sides of the Cobb-Douglas production function (and adding an error term),

$$\ln Y_t = \ln c + \alpha \ln K_t + \beta \ln L_t + \lambda t + u_t$$

The procedure is to regress $\ln Y_t$ against a constant, $\ln K_t$, $\ln L_t$, and t. The coefficient for t is an estimate of λ.

PP 4.16

Practice computer session 4.4 has the instructions for estimating the model. In terms of the model selection statistics, this model as well as the quadratic model in Practice Problem 4.15 are inferior to Model A in Table 4.2.

PP 4.18

In practice computer session 4.5 add the command *ols housing 0 gnp intrate unemp ;.* It will be seen that this model is inferior to Model A in Example 4.12 in terms of all the model selection criteria. Also, the t-statistic for *unemp* is quite low indicating that it is very insignificant.

EXERCISES

EX 4.1

If $\beta_2 = 1$, the model becomes $Y_t = \beta_1 + X_{t2} + \beta_3 X_{t3} + u_t$. Bringing X_{t2}, which has no unknown coefficient, to the left-hand side, we have $Y_t - X_{t2} = \beta_1 + \beta_3 X_{t3} + u_t$. Generate the new variable $Z_t = Y_t - X_{t2}$ and regress Z_t against a constant and X_{t3} to obtain estimates for β_1 and β_3.

EX 4.3

$$\ln E_t = \beta_1 + \beta_2 \ln Y_t + \beta_3 \ln P_t + u_t$$

(a)   The simplest form for $f(t)$ is the linear form $\beta_3 = a + bt$. Substituting this in the model we get

$$\ln E_t = \beta_1 + \beta_2 \ln Y_t + (a+bt) \ln P_t + u_t$$

34

$$= \beta_1 + \beta_2 \ln Y_t + a \ln P_t + b(t \ln P_t) + u_t$$

(b) If $b \neq 0$, then β_3 will not be constant but will be time-varying. There-fore the relevant hypotheses are $H_0: b = 0, H_1: b \neq 0$. First generate several new variables; $E2_t = \ln E_t$, $Y2_t = \ln Y_t$, $P2_t = \ln P_t$, and $P3_t = t \ln P_t$. Next regress $E2$ against a constant, $Y2, P2$, and $P3$. A straightforward t-test on the coefficient of $P3$ is applied to test whether β_2 is time-varying or not.

EX 4.4

The elasticity of Y with respect to X is $(X/Y)(dY/dX)$ (see Section 3.A.12 on elasticities). For the models listed, the expressions are, respectively, βX, $(\beta X + \gamma)/Y$, $(\beta + 2\gamma X)X/Y$, $(\beta + \gamma Z) X/Y$, and $-\beta/(XY)$.

EX 4.5

$$\text{True model:} \qquad Y_t = \beta X_t + u_t$$
$$\text{Estimated model:} \qquad Y_t = \alpha + \beta X_t + u_t$$

OLS estimator of β, using the wrong model, is given by equation (3.7) as $\hat{\beta} = S_{xy}/S_{xx}$ where S_{xx} and S_{xy} are defined in (3.8) and (3.9). $E(\hat{\beta}) = E(S_{xy})/S_{xx}$, because X is nonrandom.

$$S_{xy} = \Sigma(Y_t - \bar{Y})(X_t - \bar{X}) = \Sigma(\beta X_t + u_t - \beta\bar{X} - \bar{u})(X_t - \bar{X})$$
$$= \beta\Sigma(X_t - \bar{X})^2 + \Sigma(u_t - \bar{u})(X_t - \bar{X}) = \beta S_{xx} + S_{xu}$$

using similar notation. $E(S_{xy}) = \beta S_{xx} + E(S_{xu}) = \beta S_{xx}$ because $E(u) = 0$. Hence, $E(\hat{\beta}) = \beta$, which implies that $\hat{\beta}$ is unbiased. Thus, adding an irrelevant constant term does not bias the remaining coefficients.

EX 4.7

(a) When migration from rural to urban areas increases, some people may be unable to find employment and may either go on welfare or settle for part-time employment. This will result in an increase in the poverty rate. We will therefore expect the regression coefficient for URB to be positive. The observed sign is consistent with this intuition for all the models.

An increase in the size of the family may have two opposite effects. A larger family may have several people gainfully employed. This will increase family income and is likely to reduce the poverty rate. On the other hand, a larger family might consist mostly of children who do not generate any income. This will tend to increase the poverty rate. The observed sign is negative indicating that the former effect dominates.

One would expect that the greater the education level of a population, the lower the poverty rate. We would therefore expect a negative coefficient for all the education variables. Although the coefficients for EDUC1 and EDUC2 have the expected negative sign, the positive sign for EDUC3 is counterintuitive. It is not clear why this is so. [*Multicollinearity* is a plausible explanation but the students see this only in the next chapter.]

If the unemployment rate increases, we would expect the poverty rate also to go up. This variable has the expected positive sign.

If the median income rises, the poverty rate would be expected to drop. This is the case in all the models.

(b) The null hypothesis for the joint significance of the explanatory variables in the model is that each regression coefficient (excluding the constant term) is zero. The alternative is that at least one of the regression coefficients is nonzero. Table 4.7 has the F-statistics. For Model A, $F_c = 11.795$, $d.f. = 7,50$, and $F^*_{7,50}(0.01) = 3.035$. Because $F_c > F^*$, we reject the null hypothesis and conclude that at least one coefficient is significantly different from zero. For the remaining models, we just present the numerical values. The conclusion is the same.

Model	F_c	$d.f.$	F^*
B	14.036	6,51	3.2
C	17.144	5,52	3.4
D	20.183	4,53	3.7

(c)   The null hypothesis for a *t*-test is that a given regression coefficient is zero. The alternative for a two-tailed test is that it is not zero. The test criterion is to reject the null hypothesis if the calculated *t*-statistic is greater than a critical value. The degrees of freedom for Models A through D are, respectively, 50, 51, 52, and 53. The critical *t*-values for a two-tailed 5 percent test is approximately 2.01. A coefficient whose *t*-statistic exceeds 2.01 (in absolute value) is deemed to be significantly different from zero. The following table lists the significant variables (ignoring the constant term) for each model.

Model	Variables Significant at 5%
A	URB, MEDINC
B	URB, EDUC2, EDUC3, MEDINC
C	URB, EDUC2, EDUC3, MEDINC
D	EDUC2, EDUC3, MEDINC

It is interesting to note that URB was significant in Models A, B, and C, but is insignificant in Model D. It is, however, significant at the 10 percent level.

(d)   The null hypothesis here is that the regression coefficients for FAMSIZE and EDUC1 are zero. The alternative is that at least one of them is nonzero. The test statistic is the Wald *F*-statistic in equation (4.3). For Models A and C we have

$$F_c = \frac{(134.098-133.952)/2}{133.952/50} = 0.027$$

Under the null hypothesis, F_c has an *F*-distribution with 2 d.f. in the numerator and 50 d.f. in the denominator. $F^*(0.10) = 2.415$. Because $F_c < F^*$, we accept the null hypothesis and conclude that the regression coefficients for FAMSIZE and EDUC1 are zero. These variables are therefore candidates to be dropped.

(e) If we use the model selection criteria, a model with the lowest value for a particular selection criterion is deemed "best" for that criterion. According to this, Model C is the best because for 7 out of the 8 statistics, Model C has the lowest value. Note that this model is chosen even though UNEMP is insignificant. If significance is important, Model D should be chosen.

(f) Let the unrestricted model be

$$POVRATE = \beta_1 + \beta_2\ URB + \beta_3\ FAMSIZE + \beta_4\ EDUC\ 1$$
$$+ \beta_5\ EDUC\ 2 + \beta_6\ EDUC\ 3 + \beta_7\ UNEMP$$
$$+ \beta_8\ MEDINC + u$$

Method 1: The null hypothesis (H_0) is that $\beta_5 + \beta_6 = 0$. Under this assumption $\beta_6 = -\beta_5$. The restricted model is therefore

$$POVRATE\ =\ \beta_1 + \beta_2\ URB + \beta_3\ FAMSIZE + \beta_4\ EDUC\ 1 +$$
$$\beta_5\ EDUC\ 2 - \beta_6\ EDUC\ 3 + \beta_7\ UNEMP +$$
$$\beta_8\ MEDINC + u$$
$$=\ \beta_1 + \beta_2\ URB + \beta_3\ FAMSIZE + \beta_4\ EDUC\ 1 +$$
$$\beta_5(EDUC\ 2 - EDUC\ 3) + \beta_7 UNEMP +$$
$$\beta_8 MEDINC + u$$

First generate the new variable $Z = EDUC\ 2 - EDUC\ 3$. Next regress POVRATE against a constant URB, FAMSIZE, EDUC1, Z, UNEMP, and MEDINC to obtain the error sum of squares of the restricted model (call it ESS_R). The unrestricted model is Model A and hence its ESS is 133.952. The test statistic is

$$F_c = \frac{(ESS_R - 133.952)/1}{133.952/50}$$

which has an F-distribution (under the null hypothesis) with d.f. 1 and 50. Reject H_0 if $F_c > F^*_{1,50}(a)$ for the given level of significance a.

38

Method 2: Let $\beta = \beta_5 + \beta_6$. The null hypothesis becomes $\beta = 0$. We have, $\beta_6 = \beta - \beta_5$. Substitute this in the model.

$$
\begin{aligned}
POVRATE &= \beta_1 + \beta_2\ URB + \beta_3\ FAMSIZE + \beta_4\ EDUC1 + \\
&\quad \beta_5\ EDUC2 + (\beta-\beta_5)\ EDUC3 + \\
&\quad \beta_7\ UNEMP + \beta_8\ MEDINC + u \\
&= \beta_1 + \beta_2\ URB + \beta_3\ FAMSIZE + \beta_4\ EDUC1 + \\
&\quad \beta_5\ (EDUC2 - EDUC3) + \beta\ EDUC3 + \\
&\quad \beta_7\ UNEMP + \beta_8\ MEDINC + u
\end{aligned}
$$

Regress POVRATE against a constant, URB, FAMSIZE, EDUC1, Z, EDUC3, UNEMP, and MEDINC, and perform a *t*-test on the coefficient for EDUC3.

Method 3: Compute the following *t*-statistic

$$
t_c = \frac{\hat{\beta}_5 + \hat{\beta}_6}{[Var(\hat{\beta}_5) + Var(\hat{\beta}_6) + 2Cov(\hat{\beta}_5, \hat{\beta}_6)]^{\frac{1}{2}}}
$$

Reject $H_0: \beta_5 + \beta_6 = 0$ against $H_1: \beta_5 + \beta_6 \neq 0$ (at the 5 percent level) if $t_c > t_{50}^*(0.025)$.

(g)   Most of the important determinants of the poverty rate are already included. Other possible variables are (i) percentage of unskilled workers and (ii) average welfare payments per person or family. If a region has many unskilled workers, we can expect their earnings to be low, possibly below the poverty level. If a region has high welfare payments, it might induce immigration that increases the poverty rate.

EX 4.8

The *F*-test statistic for overall significance of a model is given by equation (4.4). We need the values of R^2, but only have $\overline{R}^2$ which is equal to 1 - $\frac{T-1}{T-k}(1 - R^2)$. Hence

$$R^2 = 1 - \frac{T-k}{T-1}(1 - \bar{R}^2)$$

From this we can calculate R^2 for the two models as 0.7023 and 0.7016. The F-statistic for the first model is 14.55 with d.f. 6 and 37. From Appendix Table A.4a, the critical F for 1 percent level is below 3.47. Because the calculated F_c is above this, we reject the null hypothesis that all regression coefficients (excepting the constant) are zero. For the second model, F_c is 22.92 which is also significant at the 1 percent level. Hence both models are extremely significant.

From the t-table at the back of the front cover, $t_{37}^*(0.025)$ and $t_{39}^*(0.025)$ are slightly below 2.042. Any regression coefficient with a t-value above this (in absolute value) is significantly different from zero. According to this, HLTH, UNEMP, and RACE have significant coefficients. For the 10 percent level, $t_{37}^*(0.05)$ and $t_{39}^*(0.05)$ are slightly below 1.697. Now the coefficient for DEP also becomes significant.

The null hypothesis to test next is that the regression coefficients for MSSEC and MPUBAS are both zero. The test statistic is given by equation (4.3). We have,

$$F_c = \frac{(ESS_B - ESS_A)/2}{ESS_A/37} = \frac{(175.524 - 175.088)/2}{175.088/37} = 0.046$$

Under the null hypothesis, this has an F-distribution with d.f. 2 for the numerator and 37 for the denominator. From Table A.4c, $F^*(2, 37)$ is slightly above 2.44 which is considerably larger than F_c. Therefore, we cannot reject the null hypothesis but conclude instead that MSSEC AND MPUBAS do not have significant effects on RETRD (given the presence of the remaining independent variables).

An increase in HLTH means a larger fraction of people is prevented from working. Such people might opt for early retirement and hence we would expect a positive coefficient for HLTH, which is the case. UNEMP might have two effects. An increase means that layoffs are higher. Companies often give inducements to employees to retire earlier in order to reduce the payroll without having to terminate employees. This will result in a positive coefficient. On the other hand, if an employee is planning to take an early retirement and seek employment elsewhere, a higher UNEMP rate would tend to discourage this. Hence RETRD is likely to be lower by this effect. The observed positive effect implies that the former effect is dominant.

Although the overall goodness of fit tests indicate that the models have good fits, only about two-third of the variation in RETRD is explained by the independent variables and hence the model could use some improvement with new variables added.

EX 4.10

$$\hat{\sigma}^2 = \frac{ESS}{T-k} = \frac{4923.914}{40-8} = 153.872$$

$$R^2 = 1 - \frac{ESS}{TSS} = 1 - \frac{4923.914}{43865.001} = 0.888$$

$$\bar{R}^2 = 1 - \frac{T-1}{T-k}(1-R^2) = 1 - \frac{39}{32}(1-0.888) = 0.863$$

The null hypothesis for overall significance is that the regression coefficients for HOME, INST, SVC, TV, AGE, AIR, and Y are all zero. The alternative is that at least one of them is not zero. The test statistic is given by equation (4.4) and has the value $F_c = 36.245$. Under the null hypothesis, F_c has the F-distribution with d.f. 7 and 32. The critical $F^*(0.01)$ is slightly below 3.30 and is less than F_c. The null hypothesis is therefore rejected.

For individual coefficients, we carry out a t-test. The critical $t_{32}^*(0.05)$ is slightly below 1.697. If the computed t_c is above this, we reject the null hypothesis that the corresponding regression coefficient is zero and conclude that the variable has a significant effect on the number of subscribers to cable TV. The following table gives the computed t_c and the criterion.

	Variable	Std. error	Test statistic	Accept/Reject
HOME	0.406	0.035	11.600	Reject
INST	- 0.526	0.476	- 1.105	Accept
SVC	2.039	2.127	0.959	Accept
TV	0.757	0.688	1.100	Accept
AGE	1.194	0.503	2.374	Reject
AIR	- 5.111	1.518	- 3.367	Reject
Y	0.0017	0.00347	0.490	Accept

The variables INST, SVC, TV, and Y are candidates to be excluded because the corresponding coefficients are not statistically significant.

For the second model, $R^2 = 0.872$ and $\bar{R}^2 = 0.862$. Both have decreased although $\bar{R}^2$ is practically the same. It would be interesting to test whether the omitted variables had *jointly significant* coefficients. The test statistic F_c is given by equation (4.3) and has the value 1.091. Under the null hypothesis, F_c has the F-distribution with d.f. 4 and 32. For a 10 percent test, F^* is slightly above 2.09. Because $F_c < F^*$, we cannot reject the hypothesis. Thus the omitted variables have coefficients that are jointly insignificant. [We could omit insignificant variables by dropping them one at a time and see if the "final" model is the same. Students may be encouraged to do this using the data in Table 4.15, which is also in the file *DATA4-15* in the accompanying diskette.]

For the t-test for individual coefficients in the second model, the critical $t^*_{36}(0.05) = 1.69$. All the regression coefficients are significantly different from zero indicating that the HOME, AGE, and AIR significantly influence the number of subscribers.

When there are more homes in an area, we would expect that the number of subscribers to cable TV will also increase and hence the regression coefficient for HOME should be positive. Older systems might have been able to help consumers overcome their initial resistance to an untested product or a new company. We would thus expect the coefficient for AGE to be positive also. We would expect the coefficient for TV to be negative because if good signals are obtained in "free" TV, the demand for "pay" TV is likely to be reduced. All three regression coefficients have the expected signs.

EX 4.11

A common alternative is to use the double-log model. First convert all the variables to logarithms and then use them in the model. Note, however, that the values of R^2 and model selection statistics are not comparable because the dependent variable is now logarithmic and not linear. To compare the results with the linear model use steps similar to those in Practice Computer Session 3.6.

EX 4.12

(a) If schooling has no effect on earnings, the coefficient for S would be zero. ($H_0 : \beta = 0$ and $H_1 : \beta \neq 0$). The test is a two-tailed t-test with 56 d.f., and $t_c = 0.094/0.005 = 18.8$. We would expect such a high t-statistic to be very significant. At the 1 percent level, $t_{56}^*(0.005)$ is only 2.7. Since $t_c > t^*$ we conclude that schooling is significant at the 1 percent level.

(b) If neither schooling nor experience have any effect on earnings, the coefficients for all the explanatory variables (except the constant) will be zero. That is the null hypothesis. The alternative is that at least one of them has a non-zero coefficient. The test is an F-test on the overall significance of the model. the test statistic is given by equation (4.4) as

$$F_c = \frac{0.337/3}{0.663/56} = 9.5$$

$F_{3,56}^*(0.01)$ is approximately 4.1, which is well below F_c. Therefore, we reject the null hypothesis and conclude that the model is significant overall.

(c) The null hypothesis is that the coefficients for N and N^2 are both zero. The alternative is that at least one of the coefficients is nonzero. Estimate the restricted model by regressing ln E against a constant and S. Then compute the F-statistic [as in equation (4.3)].

$$F_c = \frac{(ESS_R - ESS_U)/2}{ESS_U/56}$$

which has the F-distribution with 2 and 56 d.f. Reject H_0 if $F_c > F^*_{2,56}(a)$, for the level of significance a.

(d) Elasticity of E with respect to S is $(\Delta E/\Delta S)(S/E) = 0.094S$. This can be calculated provided the value of S is known. The elasticity is not constant but varies with S. Elasticity with respect to experience is $(\Delta E/\Delta N)(N/E) = N(0.023 - 0.00065N)$. This varies with N.

EX 4.13

(a) *ECSLIB* commands for part (a) are given below:

```
logs 2 3 4 5 6 ;
ols 7 0 8 9 10 11 ;
omit 8 ;
omit 10 ;
```

(b) In terms of all the model selection criteria except SGMSQ ($\hat{\sigma}^2$), Model C is the best. Also, Model C has significant regression coefficients (ignoring the constant).

(c) The null hypothesis is that the coefficients for LP, LG, LU, and LR are all insignificant. The alternative is that at least one of them is significant. We thus test the model for overall significance. The test statistic is given by equation (4.4) as

$$F_c = \frac{0.479/4}{0.521/18} = 4.14$$

which is also reported in Table 4.14. Under the null hypothesis this has an F-distribution with d.f. 4 and 18. $F_{4,18}^*(0.05) = 2.93 < F_c$. Therefore we reject the null hypothesis and conclude that the model is significant overall.

(d)   To test each regression coefficient, we use the t-test with 18 d.f. $t_{18}^*(0.025) = 2.101$. Only the coefficient for LR is higher in absolute value than this. The conclusion is that the coefficients for LG, LP, and LU are not significant. Although these appear unimportant, we should not rush to drop them all from the model simultaneously. If we do, we might run into the "omitted variable bias" problem discussed in Section 4.7. It is wise to first drop LP, which has the lowest t-value, and then reestimate the model. We note from Model B that LG now becomes significant. The reason for this drastic change in results is given in the next chapter. In Model B, LU is very insignificant and is a candidate to be eliminated. We saw earlier that the resulting model (Model C) is the best.

(e)   If the variables LP and LU are omitted from Model A, we get Model C. The test is the Wald test given in equation (4.3). We have

$$F_c = \frac{(ESS_C - ESS_A)/2}{ESS_A/18} = 0.64$$

which is less than $F_{2,18}^*(0.10) = 2.62$. Hence LP and LU are candidates for elimination. Again, we should be cautious and eliminate only LP first.

EX 4.14

(a)   As a region's income increases, we would expect the demand for labor to increase also. Income elasticity of employment is positive as expected. When the wage rate rises, the demand for labor is likely to decrease. As expected, wage elasticity is negative. If the local government spends more money, we would expect employment to go up. The elasticity for GOVTEXP is also positive as expected.

45

(b) $t_{18}^*(0.005) = 2.878$, $t_{18}^*(0.025) = 2.101$ and $t_{18}^*(0.05) = 1.734$. For significance we need $|t_c| > t^*$. At the 1 percent level, $\ln GOVTEXP$ is the only significant variable. At the 5 percent level, $\ln INCM$ is also significant, and at the 10 percent level $\ln WAGE$ is also significant. The constant term is insignificant even at the 10 percent level.

(c) When $\alpha_1 = \alpha_2$ we have,

$$\ln EMP = \alpha_0 + \alpha_1 \ln POP + \alpha_1 \ln (INCM/POP) +$$
$$\alpha_3 \ln WAGE + \alpha_4 \ln GOVTEXP + error$$
$$= \alpha_0 + \alpha_1 (\ln POP + \ln INCM - \ln POP) +$$
$$\alpha_3 \ln WAGE + \alpha_4 \ln GOVTEXP + error$$
$$= \alpha_0 + \alpha_1 \ln INCM + \alpha_3 \ln WAGE +$$
$$\alpha_4 \ln GOVTEXP + error$$

which is the original model.

$$\hat{\alpha}_1 = \hat{\alpha}_2 = 0.51, \ \hat{\alpha}_3 = -0.25, \text{ and } \hat{\alpha}_4 = 0.62.$$

(d) The wage rate is an important determinant of both the demand for and supply of labor. Hence excluding this variable will cause the "omitted variable bias." Hence, estimates and forecasts will be biased and inconsistent.

EX 4.16

(a) $\bar{R}^2 = 0.277 = 1 - (1 - R^2) \dfrac{T-1}{T-k} = 1 - (1 - R^2) \dfrac{48}{45}$ from which $R^2 = 0.322$. F_c is now obtained from equation (4.4). $F_c = 7.1 > F_{3,45}^*(.01)$ and hence the model is significant overall (more specifically, at least one of the coefficients for EDUC, EXPER, and AGE is significant).

(b) $t_{45}^*(0.025) = 2.0$ and $t_{45}^*(0.05) = 1.7$. We see that $t_c > t^*$ for EDUC and EXPER. These are significant at the 5 percent level. But $t_c < t^*$ for AGE and hence AGE is not significant even at the 10 percent level.

(c)   Other things being equal, an older person might be less productive so that the coefficient for AGE may be negative as it is here. However, because this coefficient is insignificant, the negative sign does not mean much.

(d)   This suggests a parabolic relation. An easy way to accommodate the nonlinearity is to assume that $\dfrac{\Delta WAGE}{\Delta AGE} = a + bAGE$. When AGE is smaller, $\dfrac{\Delta WAGE}{\Delta AGE}$ might be positive, whereas when AGE is large, $\dfrac{\Delta WAGE}{\Delta AGE}$ might be negative. Thus a is likely to be positive and b negative. This suggests the quadratic relation

$$WAGE = \beta_1 + \beta_2 AGE + \beta_3 AGE^2 + \beta_4 EXPER + \beta_5 EDUC + u$$

Estimate this model and test $\beta_3 = 0$ against $\beta_3 < 0$.

EX 4.17

(a) H_0 is that the coefficients for HSGPA, VSAT, and MSAT are all zero. H_1 is that at least one of the coefficients is nonzero. The test statistic is given in equation (4.4) as

$$F_c = \frac{0.22/3}{0.78/423} = 39.8$$

Under the null hypothesis this has an F-distribution with d.f. 3 and 423. The critical $F_{3,423}^*(0.01) = 3.8$ which is well below F_c. Therefore we reject the null hypothesis and conclude that at least one of the regression coefficients is nonzero.

47

(b)   A single regression coefficient is tested with a t-test. The critical t is $t^*_{423}(0.01) = 2.33$ (note that the alternative is one sided). The t-statistics for the coefficients of HSGPA, VSAT, and MSAT are obtained by dividing the corresponding regression coefficients by their standard errors. These values are 6.5, 2.6, and 3.3, all of which are above 2.33. Therefore we conclude that all the coefficients are significant at the one percent level.

(c)

$$\widehat{\Delta COLGPA} = 0.00074\ \Delta VSAT + 0.001\ \Delta MSAT = 0.074 + 0.1 = 0.174$$

The expected average increase in $COLGPA$ is therefore 0.174.

(d)   Let the general unrestricted model (U) be

$$COLGPA = \beta_1 + \beta_2\ HSGPA + \beta_3\ VSAT + \beta_4\ MSAT + u$$

The marginal effect of VSAT is β_3 and the marginal effect of MSAT is β_4. The test is therefore $\beta_3 = \beta_4$.

Method 1: Assume this condition and obtain the restricted model (R) as

$$COLGPA = \beta_1 + \beta_2\ HSGPA + \beta_3(VSAT + MSAT) + u$$

Generate the new variable $Z = VSAT + MSAT$. Next regress $COLGPA$ against a constant, $HSGPA$, and Z, and save the error of squares. The Wald F-statistic is given by equation (4.3). Reject $H_1 : \beta_3 = \beta_4$ if $F_c > F^*_{1,423}(a)$, where a is the level of significance.

Method 2: Let $\beta = \beta_3 - \beta_4$. The null hypothesis now becomes $\beta = 0$. We have $\beta_4 = \beta_3 - \beta$. Substitute this in the unrestricted model.

$$COLGPA = \beta_1 + \beta_2 HSGPA + \beta_3\ VSAT + (\beta_3 - \beta)MSAT + u$$

$$= \beta_1 + \beta_2 HSGPA + \beta_3(VSAT+MSAT) - \beta MSAT + u$$

Regress COLGPA against a constant, HSGPA, Z, and MSAT, and carry out a t-test on the coefficient of MSAT.

Method 3: The t-statistic for $\beta_3 - \beta_4$ is

$$t_c = \frac{\hat{\beta}_3 - \hat{\beta}_4}{[Var(\hat{\beta}_3) + Var(\hat{\beta}_4) - 2\,Cov(\hat{\beta}_3, \hat{\beta}_4)]^{\frac{1}{2}}}$$

Reject $H_1 : \beta_3 - \beta_4 = 0$ against $H_2 : \beta_3 - \beta_4 \neq 0$ if $t_c > t^*_{423}(a/2)$, where a is the level of significance.

(e) The major of a student is an important determinant of the GPA because some disciplines are easier to get good grades in and others are more difficult. Also, if a student went to a private school, he or she might have a better training and hence might do better in college. Thus, whether the student went to public or other types of school is important. If a student has to work for a living, then the grades are likely to suffer. Therefore the number of hours of employment might significantly affect the GPA. If a student spends a great deal of time commuting, then the grades might be lower as compared to another person who lives on campus. Not including these variables causes the "omitted variable bias" with biased and inconsistent estimates and forecasts. Furthermore, tests of hypotheses are invalid.

(f) The claim is incorrect. The dependent variable for the double-log model is $\ln(COLGPA)$ and not $COLGPA$. Therefore R^2 values are not comparable.

(g) First formulate a double-log model

$$\ln(COLGPA) = \gamma_1 + \gamma_2 \ln(HSGPA) + \gamma_3 \ln(SAT) + \gamma_4 \ln(MSAT) + v$$

The regression coefficients are now elasticities. The test procedures are similar to those in part (d).

EX 4.18
The following ECSLIB commands will be useful, in conjunction with the data file *DATA4-15*, to carry out the empirical work for this exercise.

```
ols sub const home inst svc tv age air y  ;
omit inst svc tv y  ;
logs sub home inst svc tv age air y  ;
ols l_sub const l_home l_svc l_tv l_age l_air l_y  ;
omit l_svc  ;
omit l_y  ;
```

It will be noted that the final model (which is in double-log form) has TV also with a significant elasticity and the expected positive sign.

EX 4.19
The following ECSLIB commands will be useful, in conjunction with the data file *DATA4-16*, to carry out the empirical work for this exercise.

```
ols retrd const hlth mssec mpubas unemp dep race  ;
omit mssec mpubas  ;
logs retrd hlth mssec mpubas unemp dep race  ;
ols l_retrd const l_hlth l_mssec l_mpubas l_unemp l_dep l_race  ;
omit l_mpubas  ;
omit l_dep  ;
omit l_mssec  ;
```

The final double-log model in this exercise does not have the variable DEP which the linear model in Exercise 4.8 had.

CHAPTER 5

EXERCISES

EX 5.1

The model is $y_t = \beta_2 x_{t2} + \beta_3 x_{t3} + v_t$, with $x_2 + x_3 = 1$. Substituting $x_3 = 1 - x_2$ in equation (5.3), we have

$$\hat{\beta}_2 \Sigma x_2(1 - x_2) + \hat{\beta}_3 \Sigma x_3(1 - x_2) = \Sigma y(1 - x_2)$$

$$\hat{\beta}_2 \Sigma x_2 - \hat{\beta}_2 \Sigma x_2^2 + \hat{\beta}_3 \Sigma x_3 - \hat{\beta}_3 \Sigma x_2 x_3 = \Sigma y - \Sigma y x_2$$

Because the deviation of a variable from its mean is zero (by Property 3.A.1), Σx_2, Σx_3 and Σy are zero. We readily see that the above equation reduces to equation (5.2), the first normal equation.

EX 5.2

In a double-log formulation we have, $\ln Y = \beta_1 + \beta_2 \ln X + \beta_3 \ln(X^2) + error$. But $\ln(X^2) = 2 \ln X$ and hence is exactly multicollinear with $\ln X$, which is already in the model. The steps for showing that the second normal equation reduces to the first are very similar to those in Exercise 5.1.

EX 5.4

The estimated model is $GNP = -4089.455 + 31.87\, POP$. Substituting this in Model C of Table 5.1,

$$HOUSING = -1315.750 - 184.751\, INTRATE + 14.90\, POP$$

$$+ 0.52(-4089.455 + 31.87\, POP)$$

$$= -3442.27 - 184.751\, INTRATE + 31.47\, POP$$

We note that the coefficient for POP is quite close to that of Model A. The modified constant term is much closer to the constant term than the one in Model C.

EX 5.5

(a)   The statement is wrong. Although *t*-tests might indicate individual insignificance, several variables may be jointly significant. If all the insignificant variables are dropped, we are likely to introduce serious omitted variable bias. We saw in Table 4.9 that both LG and LP are insignificant. But when LP was omitted in Model B, LG became significant. If we had eliminated both, we would have committed the specification error of omitting a variable (LG) that belongs in the model.

(b)   This statement is also wrong. Although multicollinearity (MC) does raise the standard errors, the estimates are unbiased and consistent and the *t*- and *F*-distributions are valid. Therefore the tests are valid.

EX 5.6
Yes, we would expect MC between verbal and math SAT scores as well as between HSGPA and the SAT scores, because a student who gets good grades is likely to do well in the SAT. Estimates are still unbiased, consistent, and BLUE, but might have higher standard errors. But the tests are still valid.

EX 5.7
Such a high correlation between Y and P indicates severe MC. As in Exercise 5.6, estimates are unbiased, consistent, and BLUE. Because standard errors are likely to be higher, confidence intervals are likely to be wider. Tests are, however, valid.

EX 5.8
To identify MC in Exercise 4.14, compute the correlation coefficients among the logarithms of INCM, WAGE, and GOVTEXP. If MC is present we would notice large values for these correlations. A second way to identify MC is to omit ln*WAGE* which is not significant at the 5 percent level. If the results for INCM and GOVTEXP changed drastically, MC is surely present.

In this example, it is best to ignore the MC. As pointed out in Exercise 4.14d, omitting WAGE would be a serious error in specification. Because INCM and GOVTEXP are significant even in the presence of MC, they should not be eliminated.

EX 5.9
This statement is erroneous, just the opposite is true. MC increases the standard errors and *lowers* t-statistics. A lower t-statistic is likely to make a variable insignificant rather than significant.

CHAPTER 6

PP 6.2

Let $D2 = 1$ for Democrats and 2 for Republicans. The new model is $Y = \beta_0 + \beta_1 D2 + \beta_2 X + v$. Since $D2 + D = 2$, we get $Y = \beta_0 + \beta_1(2-D) + \beta_2 X + v = (\beta_0 + 2\beta_1) - \beta_1 D + \beta_2 X + v$. We note that $\alpha_0 = \beta_0 + 2\beta_1$ and $\beta_1 = -\alpha_1$. Hence $\hat{\beta}_1 = -\hat{\alpha}_1$ and $\hat{\beta}_0 = \hat{\alpha}_0 + 2\hat{\alpha}_1$. The models are thus basically equivalent.

PP 6.3

The output for this is obtained from Practice Computer Session 6.2 (see *ps6-2.out*). In terms of the model selection criteria, the model with $\ln(SQFT)$ and *POOL* is the best in all cases. The estimated "final" model is

$$\widehat{PRICE} = -1794.475 + 278.329 \ln(SQFT) + 58.444\, POOL$$
$$(-9.35) \qquad (10.96) \qquad\qquad (3.78)$$
$$\bar{R}^2 = 0.904 \qquad\qquad d.f. = 11$$

The marginal effect of SQFT on PRICE is given by

$$\frac{\Delta \widehat{PRICE}}{\Delta SQFT} = \frac{278.329}{SQFT}$$

which, as was conjectured, decreases as *SQFT* increases.

PP 6.4

In the model $Y = \beta_1 A_1 + \beta_2 A_2 + \beta_3 A_3 + \beta X + u$, use the relation $A_3 = 1 - A_1 - A_2$. We obtain, $Y = \beta_1 A_1 + \beta_2 A_2 + \beta_3(1 - A_1 - A_2) + \beta X + u = \beta_3 + (\beta_1 - \beta_3) A_1 + (\beta_2 - \beta_3) A_2 + \beta X + u$. Therefore, $\hat{\alpha}_0 = \hat{\beta}_3$, $\hat{\alpha}_1 = \hat{\beta}_1 - \hat{\beta}_3$, and $\hat{\alpha}_2 = \hat{\beta}_2 - \hat{\beta}_3$.

PP 6.6

The values for the dummy variables are, $A_1 = 1$, $H = 1$, $E_2 = 1$, $O_3 = 1$, and zero for the others. The estimated relation is $\hat{Y} = \hat{\beta}_0 + \hat{\beta}_1 + \hat{\beta}_3 + \hat{\beta}_5 + \hat{\beta}_8 + \hat{\beta}_{10} X$.

PP 6.8

By proceeding as was done in the Analysis of Variance section we get the following 12 interdependent equations.

$$
\begin{aligned}
\mu + a_1 + b_1 &= \alpha_0 + \alpha_1 + \beta_1 \\
\mu + a_1 + b_2 &= \alpha_0 + \alpha_1 + \beta_2 \\
\mu + a_1 + b_3 &= \alpha_0 + \alpha_1 + \beta_3 \\
\mu + a_1 + b_4 &= \alpha_0 + \alpha_1 \\
\mu + a_2 + b_1 &= \alpha_0 + \alpha_2 + \beta_1 \\
\mu + a_2 + b_2 &= \alpha_0 + \alpha_2 + \beta_2 \\
\mu + a_2 + b_3 &= \alpha_0 + \alpha_2 + \beta_3 \\
\mu + a_2 + b_4 &= \alpha_0 + \alpha_2 \\
\mu + a_3 + b_1 &= \alpha_0 + \beta_1 \\
\mu + a_3 + b_2 &= \alpha_0 + \beta_2 \\
\mu + a_3 + b_3 &= \alpha_0 + \beta_3 \\
\mu + a_3 + b_4 &= \alpha_0
\end{aligned}
$$

Add all the equations and note that $\Sigma a_j = \Sigma b_k = 0$. We get $\mu = \alpha_0 + \frac{1}{3}(\alpha_1 + \alpha_2) + \frac{1}{4}(\beta_1 + \beta_2 + \beta_3)$. By adding the first four equations we can solve for a_1. By adding the next four equations a_2 can be obtained. a_3 is obtained as $-a_1 - a_2$. Once μ and a_1 are obtained, the first four equations can be used to solve for the b's.

PP 6.10

Let $D_4 = 1$ if the season is the fall and 0 otherwise. If spring is the control quarter, we use D_1, D_3, and D_4. Let $\alpha = a_0 + a_1 D_1 + a_3 D_3 + a_4 D_4$, and $\beta = b_0 + b_1 D_1 + b_3 D_3 + b_4 D_4$. The unrestricted model is now

$$E = a_0 + a_1 D_1 + a_3 D_3 + a_4 D_4 + b_0 T + b_1 D_1 T + b_3 D_3 T + b_4 D_4 T + u$$

Any hypothesis can now be formulated in terms of the a's and b's. For instance, the hypothesis that fall and spring are alike translates to the hypothesis $a_4 = b_4 = 0$, which can be tested with a Wald F-test.

PP 6.12
The intercept will be the same in all the periods if and only if $\alpha_1 = \alpha_2 = 0$. The restricted model is

$$\ln C = \alpha_0 + \beta_0 \ln P + \beta_1 (D_1 \ln P) + \cdots + u$$

The test is the familiar Wald test.

PP 6.13
The unrestricted model is now

$$\ln C = a_0 + a_2 D_2 + a_3 D_3 + b_0 \ln P + b_2(D_2 \ln P)$$

$$+ b_3(D_3 \ln P) + \cdots + u$$

Since $D_3 = D_1 - D_2$, we have

$$\ln C = a_0 + a_2 D_2 + a_3(D_1 - D_2) + b_0 \ln P$$

$$+ b_2 D_2 \ln P + b_3(D_1 - D_2) \ln P + \cdots + u$$

$$= a_0 + a_3 D_1 + (a_2 - a_3) D_2 + b_0 \ln P$$

$$+ b_3 D_1 \ln P + (b_2 - b_3) D_2 \ln P + \cdots + u$$

It follows that $a_0 = \alpha_0$, $a_3 = \alpha_1$, $a_2 - a_3 = \alpha_2$, $b_0 = \beta_0$, $b_3 = \beta_1$, and $b_2 - b_3 = \beta_2$. The a's and b's are easily estimated from the α's and β's and vice versa.

EXERCISES

EX 6.1
Suppose we exclude the years 1940 through 1945. The data used for estimation will be the 52 periods 1930-1939 and 1946-1987. Define $D = 1$ for the postwar period and 0 in the previous period. Assuming that $\alpha = \alpha_0 + \alpha_1 D$ and $\beta = \beta_0 + \beta_1 D$ we get the complete model $C = \alpha_0 + \alpha_1 D + \beta_0 Y + \beta_1(DY) + u$. The relevant test is a Wald test on $\alpha_1 = \beta_1 = 0$.

EX 6.2

(a)   The β's are the marginal effect of income on expenditure on housing. The hypothesis states that this marginal effect is the same across the three age groups.

(b)   Define two dummy variables; $D_1 = 1$ if age is between 31 and 55, 0 otherwise, and $D_2 = 1$ if age is 56 or over. The unrestricted model is

$$E = a_0 + a_1 D_1 + a_2 D_2 + b_0 Y + b_1 D_1 Y + b_2 D_2 Y + u.$$

This is estimated by regressing E against a constant, D_1, D_2, Y, and the interaction terms $D_1 Y$ and $D_2 Y$. Under the specified hypothesis, $b_1 = b_2 = 0$. Impose this restriction and regress E against a constant, D_1, D_2, and Y. Next compute F_c by equation (4.3) with $m = 2$. Reject the null hypothesis if $F_c > F^*_{2,T-6}(a)$ which is the point on $F_{2,T-6}$ to the right of which the area is a.

EX 6.3

Define the dummy variables $GENDER = 1$ for male, $RACE = 1$ for white, $CLERICAL = 1$ for clerical workers, $MAINT = 1$ for maintenance workers, and $CRAFT = 1$ for craft-oriented workers. The control group here is professionals.

Tbe basic model is

$$\ln WAGE = \alpha + \beta\,EDUC + \gamma\,EXPER + \delta\,AGE + u$$

Let

$$\alpha = \alpha_0 + \alpha_1\,GENDER + \alpha_2\,RACE + \alpha_3\,CLERICAL + \alpha_4\,MAINT + \alpha_5\,CRAFT$$

and similarly for β, γ, and δ. Substituting these in the basic model we get the complete unrestricted model as (Model U).

$$\ln WAGE = \alpha_0 + \alpha_1 GENDER + \alpha_2 RACE + \alpha_3 CLERICAL$$
$$+ \alpha_4 MAINT + \alpha_5 CRAFT$$
$$+ EDUC\,(\beta_0 + \beta_1 GENDER + \beta_2 RACE$$

57

$$+ \beta_3 CLERICAL + \beta_4 MAINT + \beta_5 CRAFT)$$

$$+ EXPER\ (\gamma_0 + \gamma_1 GENDER + \gamma_2 RACE$$

$$+ \gamma_3 CLERICAL + \gamma_4 MAINT + \gamma_5 CRAFT)$$

$$+ AGE\ (\delta_0 + \delta_1 GENDER + \delta_2 RACE$$

$$+ \delta_3 CLERICAL + \delta_4 MAINT + \delta_5 CRAFT) + u$$

To carry out the empirical analysis for this question, first copy the input file *ps6-5.inp* as *ex6-3.inp*. Next delete the line *quit* and add the following lines (it is convenient to use the text editor program *edit* included in the program diskette).

```
(*  save ESS and d.f. for Exercise 6.3b (ii) and (iii)  *)
genr ESSU = $ess
genr DFU = $df
(*  Wald F-test for Exercise 6.3b (i)  *)
omit GENDER RACE EXP_GEN EXP_RACE AGE_GEN
 AGE_RACE ;
(*  Create new variable needed for Wald F-test for Exercise 6.3b (ii)  *)
genr Z = EXP_GEN + EXP_RACE
(*  estimate restricted model using Z instead of EXP_GEN
 and EXP_RACE  *)
ols LWAGE const EDUC EXPER AGE GENDER RACE CLERICAL
 MAINT CRAFTS sq_EDUC sq_EXPER sq_AGE ED_GEN
 ED_RACE ED_CLER ED_MAINT ED_CRAFT AGE_GEN
 AGE_RACE AGE_CLER AGE_MAIN AGE_CRFT Z EXP_CLER
 EXP_MAIN EXP_CRFT ;
(*  save ESSR, compute F-statistic and its p-value  *)
genr ESSR = $ess
genr Fc = (ESSR - ESSU)*DFU/ESSU
pvalue 4 1 DFU Fc
(*  Create new variables needed for Wald F-test for Exercise 6.3b (iii)  *)
genr Z1 = GENDER + RACE
genr Z2 = EDUC*Z1
```

```
genr Z3 = AGE*Z1
genr Z4 = EXPER*Z1
(* estimate restricted model using the Z's *)
ols LWAGE const EDUC EXPER AGE Z1 CLERICAL MAINT
 CRAFTS sq_EDUC sq_EXPER sq_AGE Z2 ED_CLER
 ED_MAINT ED_CRAFT Z3 AGE_CLER AGE_MAIN AGE_CRFT
 Z3 EXP_CLER EXP_MAIN EXP_CRFT ;
(* save NEW ESSR, compute F-statistic and its p-value *)
genr ESSR = $ess
genr Fc = (ESSR - ESSU)*DFU/ESSU
pvalue 4 4 DFU Fc
```

Finally execute this batch file using the ECSLIB command

$$\text{ecslib data6-9} < \text{ex6-3.inp} > \text{ex6-3.out}$$

(i)   If $EDUC = 0$ for two employees, the model for them is Model R without the EDUC terms. The hypothesis now becomes $\alpha_1 = \alpha_2 = \gamma_1 = \gamma_2 = \delta_1 = \delta_2 = 0$. This is done with the familiar Wald F-test. [Note that β_1 and β_2 are not included here because we are considering two employees with no education.]

The Wald F-statistic for the above test is $F_c = 0.6245$ which has the F-distribution with d.f. 6 and 22. The p-value for this is 0.708868 which is unacceptably high. We therefore cannot reject the null hypothesis.

(ii) The marginal effect of experience is
$$\gamma = \gamma_0 + \gamma_1 GENDER + \gamma_2 RACE + \gamma_3 CLERICAL + \gamma_4 MAINT + \gamma_5 CRAFT$$
For white females this is
$$\gamma_0 + \gamma_2 + \gamma_3 CLERICAL + \gamma_4 MAINT + \gamma_5 CRAFT$$
For non-white males this is
$$\gamma_0 + \gamma_1 + \gamma_3 CLERICAL + \gamma_4 MAINT + \gamma_5 CRAFT$$

These two marginal effects will be equal if and only if $\gamma_1 = \gamma_2$ (note that

59

we do not require them to be equal to zero). The procedure for testing this is similar to that in Example 4.9. The value of F_c for this is 0.317206 with the p-value 0.578987 which is also high. Therefore, we accept the null hypothesis specified here also.

(iii) First write down Model U separately for white females and non-white males. Then identify the condition under which these two relations will be identical (verify that it is $\alpha_1 = \alpha_2$, $\beta_1 = \beta_2$, $\gamma_1 = \gamma_2$, and $\delta_1 = \delta_2$). Next impose these restrictions and get the restricted Model R. Finally, use the Wald F-test to test these four restrictions. The d.f. are 4 and $T-k$, where k is the number of parameters in the unrestricted model. The empirical value of $F_c = 3.528521$ and the corresponding p-value is 0.02272. The null hypothesis is therefore rejected.

EX 6.5

(a) If there are more competing stations in the same area, a given station's market share will decrease. We can therefore expect $\dfrac{\partial SHARE}{\partial STAT}$ to be negative. If more households are wired for cable, the demand for a commercial television's programs is likely to decrease. Hence $\dfrac{\partial SHARE}{\partial CABLE} < 0$. An increase in income is likely to increase the overall demand for television but there is no reason to expect that a particular station's share will be affected. That is, $\dfrac{\partial SHARE}{\partial INCOME} = 0$.

(b) Let $VHF = 1$ if the t-th station is VHF and 0 otherwise. Let $ABC = 1$ if the station is affiliated with ABC, and 0 otherwise. Similarly, let $CBS = 1$ for a CBS station and 0 otherwise. Let $NBC = 1$ for an NBC affiliated station. The control group consists of those not affiliated with ABC, NBC, or CBS.

(i) Let $\alpha = \alpha_0 + \alpha_1 UHF + \alpha_2 ABC + \alpha_3 CBS + \alpha_4 NBC$. The null hypothesis $\alpha_1 = \alpha_2 = \alpha_3 = \alpha_4 = 0$ is tested by a Wald F-test.

(ii)   Let $\beta = \beta_0 + \beta_1 UHF + \cdots$, and similarly for γ and δ. The null hypothesis $\alpha_1 = \beta_1 = \gamma_1 = \delta_1 = \cdots = 0$ (excluding α_0, β_0, and δ_0) is tested by the Wald test.

EX 6.6

Because there are six geographic regions, we define 5 dummy variables, say NW, SW, NC, SC, and NE. NW = 1 for states in the northwest and 0 elsewhere, and similarly for the other regions. The rest of the analysis very closely parallels the second hypothesis in Exercise 6.4.

EX 6.7

Let $URBAN = 1$ if a household is in the urban area and 0 elsewhere. First stack the data (see Section 6.6) on each of the variables and get new variables EXP, Y, N, $Z_1 = Y \times URBAN$, and $Z_2 = N \times URBAN$. The complete model is now

$$EXP = a_0 + a_1 URBAN + b_0 Y + b_1 Z_1 + c_0 N + c_0 Z_2 + u$$

(i) $\alpha_0 = \beta_0$ is equivalent to $a_0 = 0$. This is done with a t-test on a_0.

(ii) $\alpha_0 = \beta_0$ is tested with a t-test on b_0.

(iii) $\alpha_2 = \beta_2$ is tested with a t-test on c_0.

(iv)   This is tested with a joint F-test (Wald test) on $a_0 = b_0 = c_0 = 0$.

EX 6.8

(a)   The null hypothesis is that the coefficient for DCAM is zero. The alternative is that it is not zero. The t-statistic for Model A is $t_c = -0.041/0.052 = -0.788$. Because $|t_c| < t^*_{417}(0.05)$, the coefficient is insignificant at the 10 percent level. The same result holds for Model D also.

(b)   The null hypothesis is that the coefficient for DPUB is zero and the alternative is that it is nonzero. For Model A, $t_c = 0.029/0.063 = 0.46$. This is also very small indicating insignificance.

(c) The null hypothesis is that the coefficients for DSCI, DSOC, DHUM, and DARTS are all zero. The alternative is that at least one of the coefficients is nonzero. The unrestricted model is Model A. The restricted model is Model D. The test statistic is

$$F_c = \frac{(ESS_D - ESS_A)/4}{ESS_A/417} = 0.789$$

Under the null hypothesis, $F_c \sim F_{4,417}$. $F_{4,417}^*(0.1) = 1.94$ which is greater than F_c. We therefore accept the null hypothesis and conclude that the major does not matter in determining COLGPA. When Model B is the unrestricted model, Model C becomes the restricted model. $F_c = 0.807$ which is also insignificant.

(d) We have,

$$F_c = \frac{(ESS_C - ESS_A)/6}{ESS_A/417} = 0.694$$

This too is insignificant. The conclusion is that none of the dummy variables have significant coefficients.

EX 6.9

Define new dummy variables, $PROF = 1$ for a professor, 0 for others, $ASSOC = 1$ for an associate professor, 0 for others (assistant professors being the control group), $OPP = 1$ if the opportunity for promotion is good, $SPOUSE = 1$ if the spouse has a good opportunity for employment, and $HAPPY = 1$ if the professor is happy with the administration.

(a) The unrestricted model is

$$AVGYR = \alpha_0 + \alpha_1 ASSOC + \alpha_2 PROF + \alpha_3 OPP + \alpha_4 HAPPY$$

$$+ \alpha_5 SPOUSE + \beta PAPERS + \gamma AGE + u$$

The null hypothesis is $\alpha_1 = \alpha_2 = \alpha_3 = \alpha_4 = \alpha_5 = 0$ and the restricted model is

$$AVGYR = \alpha_0 + \beta PAPERS + \gamma AGE + u$$

The test is the Wald test using equation (4.3).

(b)   We write

$$\beta = \beta_0 + \beta_1 ASSOC + \cdots$$

$$\gamma = \gamma_0 + \gamma_1 ASSOC + \cdots$$

The null hypothesis is that $\alpha_i = \beta_i = \gamma_i = 0$ for $i = 1, 2, 3, 4, 5$. The usual Wald test is the appropriate one.

EX 6.10

Define $D_1 = 1$ for one with a bachelor's degree, 0 otherwise, and $D_2 = 1$ for one with a post-graduate degree, 0 otherwise.

(a)   The basic model is $E = \alpha + \beta N + u$. Let $\alpha = a_0 + a_1 D_1 + a_2 D_2$ and $\beta = b_0 + b_1 D_1 + b_2 D_2$. The unrestricted model becomes

$$E = a_0 + a_1 D_1 + a_2 D_2 + b_0 N + b_1 (ND_1) + b_2 (ND_2) + u$$

(b)   Because all the observations are pooled together, the size of the sample will be considerably larger than that in a single group. As we note in Chapter 3, the larger the number of observations (or d.f.) the lower the variance of an estimate and the higher the power of a test. Lower variance means greater efficiency.

(c)   The models for groups B and C are:

   (B) $E = (a_0 + a_1) + (b_0 + b_1)N + u$

   (C) $E = (a_0 + a_2) + (b_0 + b_2)N + u$

The relations will be identical if and only if $a_0 = a_2$ and $b_0 = b_2$. This will be the null hypothesis and the alternative is that at least one of the restrictions does not hold. First estimate the unrestricted model. When the restrictions are imposed we get the model

$$E = a_0 + a_1(D_1 + D_2) + b_0 N + b_1 N(D_1 + D_2) + u$$

Compute F_c using equation (4.3) with $m = 2$, $k = 6$, and $T =$ the size of the pooled sample. Under the null hypothesis F_c has an F-distribution with d.f. 2 and $T-6$. Reject H_0 if $F_c > F^*_{2,T-6}(a)$, where a is the level of significance and F^* is the point on $F_{2,T-6}$ such that the area to the right is a.

63

EX 6.11

(a) The larger the population the greater the number of cars, buses, planes, and other transportation equipment that cause air pollution. Value added is an indicator of economic activity and hence can be expected to contribute to air pollution. Rain usually clears the air and hence can be expected to impro᷄ ᷄ir quality. Population density would have the same effect as population. Median income is also an indicator of economic activity that often worsens air quality. The poverty level of an SMSA is not likely to affect air quality. ELECTR, FUELOIL, INDESTAB, are all indicators of economic activity. We would expect them to contribute adversely to air quality.

(b)

$$AIRQUAL = \beta_0 + \beta_1 VALADD + \beta_2 RAIN + \beta_3 DENSITY$$
$$+ \beta_4 MEDINCM + \beta_5 ELECTR$$
$$+ \beta_6 FUELOIL + \beta_7 INESTAB + u$$

Population is excluded because the density of population is included. Poverty rate is excluded because it does not appear to be relevant. The estimated model is (*t*-statistics in parenthesis)

$$\widehat{AIRQUAL} = \underset{(4.84)}{97.160} + \underset{(0.50)}{0.002\,VALADD} - \underset{(-0.07)}{0.032\,RAIN}$$
$$\underset{(-0.36)}{- 0.000748\,DENSITY} - \underset{(-0.04)}{0.000104\,MEDINCM}$$
$$\underset{(0.27)}{+ 0.052\,ELECR} + \underset{(0.54)}{0.000946\,FUELOIL}$$
$$\underset{(-0.05)}{- 0.001\,INDESTAB}$$

$$R^2 = 0.138 \quad \bar{R}^2 = -0.136 \quad F = 0.505 \quad d.f. = 22$$

The negative value for $\bar{R}^2$ indicates a poor model. It can be verified that the low *F*-statistic indicates that the overall significance of the model is very poor.

(c) Yes, we would expect multicollinearity problems. For instance, the correlation between INDESTAB and MEDINC is 0.986 which is almost perfect. The correlation between INDESTAB and VALADD is 0.921. As we know from Chapter 5, multicollinearity lowers t-statistics and is likely to make regression coefficients insignificant. This certainly appears to be the case here.

(d) For simplicity, we assume that only the constant is affected by the dummy variable COAST. Coastal SMSA's frequently have winds from off$F$-shore which clear up air pollution. We might therefore expect a negative coefficient for COAST. Empirically this result holds with a strong t-statistic.

(e) By eliminating insignificant variables in a step by step fashion, the "final model" was obtained as follows:

$$\widehat{AIRQUAL} = 122.258 + 0.0026 \; FUELOIL - 33.497 \; COAST$$
$$\qquad\qquad (15.7) \qquad (2.4) \qquad\qquad\qquad (-3.6)$$

$$\bar{R}^2 = 0.324 \qquad F = 7.963 \qquad d.f. = 27$$

The F-statistic is significant at the level 0.0019 and $\bar{R}^2$ is positive. It is interesting to note that all the economic activity variables thought to be important a priori are empirically insignificant. Air quality depends mainly on the amount of fuel oil used and whether an SMSA is on the coast or not.

(f) A number of transportation variables could be entered directly; numbers of automobiles, trucks, and planes; number of gallons of gasoline consumed. Another variable is the number of tons of solid waste burned in sewage plants and solid waste incinerators.

EX 6.12
Using the DOS command *edit ex6-12.inp*, create an ECSLIB command input file with the following lines:

(* EX 6.12, using DATA6-11, for Exercise 6.12 *)

```
genr lsqft = log(sqft)
ols price const sqft lsqft yard ;
(* compute the marginal effect of sqft on price *)
genr DPDSQFT = coeff(sqft) + (coeff(lsqft)/sqft)
graph DPDSQFT sqft ;
(* kitchen sink model with all the characteristics of a home *)
ols price const sqft lsqft yard age aircon baths bedrms cond corner
 culd dish fence firepl floors garage irreg lajolla lndry patio pool
 rooms sprink view ;
(* omit variables with high p-values *)
omit age aircon bedrms cond corner dish floors garage patio ;
omit culd fence ;
omit rooms ;
omit lndry pool ;
```

Then run this with the following command and study the output file.

ecslib data6-11 < ex6-12.inp > ex6-12.out

The basic model does not have a good fit because it explains only 45.5 percent of the variation in the price of homes. The regression coefficients are all significant at levels below 1.5 percent. The marginal effect of SQFT on PRICE is given by

$$\frac{\Delta PRICE}{\Delta SQFT} = \beta + \frac{\gamma}{SQFT} = 0.34218 - \frac{501.64495}{SQFT}$$

The graph of this relationship (see the output file *ex6-12.out*) indicates that the marginal effect is negative at low values of SQFT, but increases steadily as SQFT increases. This is counterintuitive and might be because the marginal effect holds other variables constant which is not realistic. For instance, the size of the yard is not the same between a home with SQFT 950 and another with SQFT 3,500.

The complete model explains about 70 percent of the variation in price. However, many of the regression coefficients have very high *p*-values indicating insignificance. After omitting these, a few at a time, the "final" model explains about 76.8 percent of the variation in price. The significance of the variables are as follows, and all have expected signs:

1 percent :	SQFT, LSQFT, LA JOLLA
1-5 percent :	YARD, IRREG, SPRINK
5-10 percent :	BATHS, FIREPL, VIEW, LNDRY, POOL

EX 6.13

(a) To compute ESS, note that $\hat{\sigma}^2 = ESS/(T-k)$. Hence $ESS_A = 1.275(106-15) = 116.025$, $ESS_B = 118.243$, and $ESS_C = 120.05$. For Model B, the null hypothesis is that the coefficients for LENGTH, WIDTH, DEFOG, FOURDOOR, HATCH, and DIESEL are all zero. The alternative is that at least one of the coefficients is nonzero.

$$F_c = \frac{(118.243 - 116.025)/6}{116.025/91} = 0.29$$

which is well below $F^*_{6,91}(0.10)$. We therefore accept the null hypothesis.

For Model C, the null hypothesis is that the coefficients for LENGTH, WIDTH, LITERS, DEFOG, FOURDOOR, HATCH, and DIESEL are all zero. The alternative is that at least one of them is non-zero.

$$F_c = \frac{(120.05 - 116.025)/7}{116.025/91} = 0.45$$

which is well below $F^*_{7,91}(0.10)$. Here also we accept the null hypothesis.

(b) According to all but $\hat{\sigma}^2$, Model C is the "best" because it has lower values for the selection statistics. All the remaining regression coefficients have high t-values indicating significance. The dependent variable is the list price of a car which is closely related to the cost of production rather than the demand for the product. We would generally expect positive coefficients except for CARB. Carburator-equipped cars are likely to be cheaper. WBASE and HEIGHT have unexpected negative signs which are counterintuitive. The magnitude of the CRUZ is unbelievably high ($5,705). It might be a proxy for a number of options not included in the analysis (sun roof, power windows, etc.).

CHAPTER 7

EXERCISES

EX 7.1

Using the text editor *edit* (or some or other word-processing program) create a file called *ex7-1.inp* that contains the following lines.

```
(*  EX7.1, using DATA6-1, for Exercise 7.1  *)
genr lsqft = log(sqft)  ;
(*  estimate basic model  *)
ols price const sqft  ;
(*  save residuals  *)
genr ut=uhat
(*  estimate auxiliary regression with ut as the dependent variable  *)
ols ut const sqft lsqft bedrms baths pool famroom firepl  ;
(*  compute TR-square statistic  *)
genr trsq =$nobs*$rsq
(*  compute pvalue for it  *)
pvalue 3 6 trsq
(*  estimate a new model with the "candidate" variables added  *)
ols price const sqft lsqft bedrms pool  ;
(*  omit variable with highest pvalue and reestimate model  *)
omit sqft  ;
omit bedrms  ;
(*  compare with Model F in Table 6.2  *)
ols price const sqft pool ;
```

Next estimate the relevant models using the following command and study the output file *ex7-1.out*.

```
ecslib  data6-1  <  ex7-1.inp  >  ex7-2.out
```

The first step is to estimate the basic model by regressing PRICE against a constant and SQFT. Then save the residuals as $\hat{u}_t$. In Practice Problem 6.3 we saw that the logarithm of SQFT was a better explanatory variable than SQFT. For this reason, we created the variable LSQFT = ln(SQFT). The auxiliary regression (presented below) consists of regressing $\hat{u}_t$ against a constant, SQFT, LSQFT, BEDROOMS, BATHS, POOL, FAMROOM, and FIREPL.

VARIABLE	COEFFICIENT	STDERROR	T STAT	PROB t > |T|	
CONSTANT	-3575.22406	1984.00975	-1.802	0.1216	
SQFT	-0.25727	0.14984	-1.717	0.1368	
LSQFT	553.60971	308.12457	1.797	0.1225	
BEDRMS	-24.95049	26.93879	-0.926	0.3901	
BATHS	8.54326	36.43601	0.234	0.8224	
POOL	57.58217	19.37061	2.973	0.0249	**
FAMROOM	-23.21958	37.35502	-0.622	0.5571	
FIREPL	-28.01834	55.76284	-0.502	0.6333	

Unadjusted R-squared for the above regression is 0.679, which gives TR^2 = 9.506. Under the null hypothesis that the coefficients for the added variables are all zero, this test statistic has the Chi-square distribution with 6 d.f. The p-value for this is 0.15, which is unacceptably high and hence we cannot reject the null hypothesis. Although the conclusion appears to be that none of the new variables has a significant effect, the p-value for the coefficient for POOL indicates significance at the 2.49 percent level. We therefore note that the strict TR^2 test might "fail" in the sense that it might reject the maintained null hypothesis although some individual coefficients might be significant or nearly significant. This is where the auxiliary regression becomes even more useful. We should use it to select "candidate" variables to be included in the original model *regardless of the result of the TR^2 test*. Strict significance would suggest that only POOL should be included. However, this rule would miss variables which might be insignificant because of multicollinearity (for example between SQFT and LSQFT). A more conservative rule is to choose variables with *p*-values under 0.50 (the choice is arbitrary and others might prefer to use a different value such as 0.25 or 0.30). It should be noted that the coefficients and *p*-values for the variables in the *original basic model* (CONSTANT and SQFT in our case) are irrelevant here and should be ignored.

According to the conservative rule proposed here, LSQFT, BEDROOMS, and POOL will be included in the original formulation and a new model estimated. Thereafter, the procedure is the same as before, namely, omit variables with highest *p*-values (a few at a time to be on the safe side) until no insignificant coefficients are present. In our case, the final model with the "best" model selection statistics is the one with a constant term, log of SQFT, and POOL.

EX 7.2
Create a file called *ex7-2.inp* with the following ECSLIB commands.

```
(*  EX 7.2, using DATA6-11, for Exercise 7.2  *)
genr lsqft = ln(sqft)
(*  Estimate basic model  *)
ols price const sqft lsqft yard  ;
(*  save the residuals  *)
genr ut = uhat
(*  estimate the auxiliary regression  *)
ols ut const sqft lsqft yard age aircon baths bedrms cond corner culd
 dish fence firepl floors garage irreg lajolla lndry patio pool
 rooms sprink view  ;
(*  compute TRsquare  *)
genr trsq = $nobs*$rsq
(*  compute the p-value  *)
pvalue 3 20 trsq
(*  include variables with p-values < 0.5 in the auxiliary regression  *)
ols price const sqft lsqft yard baths culd fence firepl irreg lajolla
 lndry pool rooms sprink view  ;
(*  omit insignificant terms  *)
```

omit culd fence ;
omit rooms ;

Then execute the program using the following DOS command and study the output file *ex7-2.out*.

ecslib data6-11 < ex7-2.inp > ex7-2.out

The value of TR^2 is $59 \times 0.658 = 38.8$ which has a Chi-square distribution with 20 d.f. under the null hypothesis that the added variables have insignificant effects. It is easy to verify that the test statistic is extremely significant. The auxiliary regression suggests the inclusion of the variables *baths, culd, fence, firepl, irreg, lajolla, lndry, pool, rooms, sprink,* and *view* in the original model. If we omit insignificant variables, a few at a time, we end up with the same "final" model as in Exercise 6.12. Thus, in this example, the Hendry/LSE approach of going from the general to the simple yields the same ultimate model as the LM test approach that starts with a basic model and adds new variables. It should be cautioned that such a nice result need not always hold and hence it would be wise to use both approaches to obtain robust results.

EX 7.3
First create a text file called *ex7-3.inp* with the following ECSLIB commands.

```
(* EX 7.3, using DATA6-9, for Exercise 7.3 *)
logs WAGE EDUC EXPER AGE ;
(* estimate basic double-log model and save the residuals *)
ols l_WAGE const l_EDUC l_EXPER l_AGE ;
genr ut = uhat
(* The following transformations generate interactions *)
genr LED_GEN=l_EDUC*GENDER
genr LED_RACE=l_EDUC*RACE
genr LED_CLER=l_EDUC*CLERICAL
genr LED_MAIN=l_EDUC*MAINT
genr LED_CRFT=l_EDUC*CRAFTS
```

71

```
genr LAGE_GEN=l_AGE*GENDER
genr LAGE_RAC=l_AGE*RACE
genr LAGE_CLR=l_AGE*CLERICAL
genr LAGE_MAI=l_AGE*MAINT
genr LAGE_CRF=l_AGE*CRAFTS
genr LEXP_GEN=l_EXPER*GENDER
genr LEXP_RAC=l_EXPER*RACE
genr LEXP_CLR=l_EXPER*CLERICAL
genr LEXP_MAI=l_EXPER*MAINT
genr LEXP_CRF=l_EXPER*CRAFTS
list
(* The following is the auxiliary regression *)
ols ut const l_EDUC l_EXPER l_AGE LED_GEN LED_RACE
 LED_CLER LED_MAIN LED_CRFT LAGE_GEN LAGE_RAC
 LAGE_CLR LAGE_MAI LAGE_CRF LEXP_GEN LEXP_RAC
 LEXP_CLR LEXP_MAI LEXP_CRF ;
(* compute TRsquare and the p-value *)
genr trsq = $nobs*$rsq
pvalue 3 15 trsq
(* estimate model with selected variables added  *)
ols l_WAGE const l_EDUC l_EXPER l_AGE LED_GEN
 LED_RACE LED_CLER LED_MAIN LED_CRFT LAGE_GEN
 LAGE_RAC LAGE_MAI LAGE_CRF LEXP_GEN LEXP_RAC
 LEXP_CLR LEXP_MAI LEXP_CRF ;
(* omit insignificant terms a few at a time  *)
omit LEXP_CRF LED_RACE LED_GEN ;
omit LAGE_GEN LAGE_CRF ;
omit LAGE_MAI LEXP_MAI ;
```

Execute the above with the DOS command

$$ecslib \ \ data6\text{-}9 \ < \ ex7\text{-}3.inp \ > \ ex7\text{-}3.out$$

The value of TR^2 is $49 \times 0.813 = 39.8$ which has a Chi-square distribution with 15 d.f. under the null hypothesis that the added variables have insignificant effects. It is easy to verify that the test statistic is extremely significant. The next step is to select variables from the auxiliary regression, estimate a new model, and then eliminate those with insignificant regression coefficients. The "final" model obtained by this procedure is the following (the dependent variable is ln WAGE).

VARIABLE	COEFFICIENT	STDERROR	T STAT	PROB t > |T|
constant	7.43818	0.37954	19.598	< 0.0001 ***
1_EDUC	0.34166	0.06046	5.651	< 0.0001 ***
1_EXPER	0.20413	0.07877	2.591	0.0135 **
1_AGE	-0.23667	0.12395	-1.909	0.0638 *
LED_CLER	-0.35156	0.05278	-6.661	< 0.0001 ***
LED_MAIN	-0.29077	0.05295	-5.491	< 0.0001 ***
LED_CRFT	-0.13278	0.04239	-3.133	0.0033 ***
LAGE_RAC	0.16174	0.05195	3.113	0.0035 ***
LEXP_GEN	0.11723	0.03054	3.839	0.0005 ***
LEXP_RAC	-0.23047	0.08607	-2.678	0.0109 **
LEXP_CLR	0.09130	0.05628	1.622	0.1130

Unadjusted R-squared   0.824   Adjusted R-squared   0.777

F-statistic (10, 38)   17.769   Prob. F > 17.769 = < 0.00001

The variables in the above model explain about 77.7 percent of the variation in the logarithm of WAGE. The elasticity of wage with respect to education is given by

$$\frac{\Delta \widehat{ln(WAGE)}}{\Delta ln(EDUC)} = 0.342 - 0.352\, CLERICAL - 0.291\, MAIN - 0.133\, CRAFT$$

As can be expected, the elasticity is lower for clerical, maintenance, and craft workers as compared to professional workers. There is no significant interaction due to gender and race.

Not surprisingly, the elasticity of wage with respect to age is negative as shown below.

$$\frac{\Delta ln\,(WAGE)}{\Delta ln\,(AGE)} = -0.237 + 0.162\,RACE$$

It interacts significantly only with race, with white employees having a smaller numerical value for the elasticity.

Experience has the expected positive effect (see below), but being non-white implies a lower value for the elasticity.

$$\frac{\Delta ln\,(WAGE)}{\Delta ln\,(EXPER)} = 0.204 + 0.117\,GENDER - 0.230\,RACE + 0.091\,CLERICAL$$

EX 7.5

First estimate the basic model in equation (6.28) and save the residuals $\hat{u}_t$. Next regress $\hat{u}_t$ against the unrestricted model presented in Section 6.5 (it has all the dummy variables and interaction terms) and compute R^2. Under the null hypothesis that the added variables have coefficients which are zero, TR^2 has a chi-square distribution with 6 d.f. Reject H_o if TR^2 exceeds the critical χ_6^2.

The p-values for the added variables will be useful in selecting possible variables to include. Although there is no strict rule for selection, a p-value less than 0.5 is a useful cut-off.

EX 7.6

First define 23 dummy variables $D_i = 1$ during the i-th hour of the day, 0 otherwise (the choice of control is arbitrary; perhaps hour 3 could be used). Next generate $Z_i = D_i \times T$ which is the interaction between D_i and T. Then estimate the basic model $E_t = a + b\,T_t + u_t$ and save $\hat{u}_t$. Estimate the auxiliary regression $\hat{u}_t$ against a constant, T_t, all the dummies (D_i) and the interactions (Z_i), and compute R^2. Under the null hypothesis that there is no time-of-day difference in the relation, $TR^2 \sim \chi_{46}^2$. Reject H_o if TR^2 exceeds the critical χ_{46}^2. Again, the t-statistics in the auxiliary regression will be useful guides for selecting possible variables for inclusion in the model.

74

EX 7.8

First study the answer to Exercise 6.5. The procedure, as before, is to estimate the basic model and save $\hat{u}_t$. Then estimate the auxiliary regression with $\hat{u}_t$ as the dependent variable and all the independent variables in the unrestricted model. For part (i) of Exercise 6.5(b) TR^2 will be χ_4^2. Reject H_o if TR^2 exceeds the critical χ_4^2. For part (ii), the procedure is the same but $TR^2 \sim \chi_{16}^2$.

EX 7.9

First regress WLFP against a constant, YF, EDUC, UE, URB, and WH, and save $\hat{u}_t$. Then generate the dummy variables and interactions described in the answers to Exercise 6.6. Regress $\hat{u}_t$ against all the independent variables in the unrestricted model. TR^2 will now be χ_{30}^2. The test is conducted in the usual way (see answers to previous questions).

EX 7.10

As the procedure is similar, we provide only a brief sketch. Regress ln (PTM) against a constant, ln(WT), PD, and ln(DIST), and save $\hat{u}_t$. Regress $\hat{u}_t$ against these variables plus all the dummy variables and interactions and compute R^2. Then perform the TR^2 test.

CHAPTER 8

EXERCISES

EX 8.2

(a)   The density function for u_t is $\dfrac{1}{\Sigma\sqrt{2\pi}}\, e^{-u_t^2/(2\sigma_t^2)}$. The likelihood function is therefore

$$L = \frac{1}{\sigma^T (2\pi)^{T/2}}\, e^{-\Sigma u_t^2/(2\sigma_t^2)}$$

Logarithm of this gives

$$\ln L = -T \ln \sigma - T \ln (\sqrt{2\pi}) - \Sigma \frac{u_t^2}{2\sigma_t^2}$$

Substituting for u_t from the model we get the desired answer.

(b)   When $\sigma_t^2 = \sigma^2 Z_t^2$, the log likelihood function becomes

$$\ln L = -T\ln \sigma - T\ln (\sqrt{2\pi}) - \Sigma \left[\frac{(Y_t - \beta_1 - \beta_2 X_{t1} - \beta_3 X_{t2})^2}{2\sigma^2 Z_t^2} \right]$$

Maximizing $\ln L$ is equivalent to minimizing

$$\Sigma \left[\frac{Y_t - \beta_1 - \beta_2 X_{t2} - \beta_3 X_{t3}}{Z_t} \right]^2 =$$

$$\Sigma(w_t\, Y_t - \beta_1\, w_t - \beta_2\, w_t\, X_{t2} - \beta_3\, w_t\, X_{t3})^2$$

where $w_t = 1/Z_t$. This gives the WLS estimates of Exercise 11.1.

EX 8.4

It is known that $\sigma_t^2 = \sigma^2 Z_t$. The weight for WLS is inversely proportional to the standard deviation of the error terms. Therefore $w_t = 1/\sqrt{Z_t}$. Multiply each variable by w_t and use the transformed variables in the regression.

EX 8.5

Only the housing example is examined here. The procedure is similar for the automobile expenditure example. Because population is growing over time, there is no need to rearrange the observations. To obtain the output to verify the answers given here, create a text file (call it *ex8-5.inp*) with the following ECSLIB commands.

```
(*  EX 8.5, using DATA4-11, for Exercise 8.5  *)
smpl 1963 1970
(*  G-Q test calculations  *)
ols housing 0 intrate gnp ;
smpl 1978 1985
ols housing 0 intrate gnp ;
genr df=$df
genr GQFc = 17815/17415
print GQFc ;
pvalue 4 df df GQFc
(*  B-P test calculations  *)
smpl 1963 1985
ols housing 0 intrate gnp ;
genr T = $nobs
genr usq=uhat*uhat
genr sgmasq = $ess/T
genr bpusq=usq/sgmasq
genr popsq=pop*pop
ols bpusq 0 popsq ;
genr sy = sd(bpusq)
genr tss = (T-1)*sy*sy
genr bptest = $rsq * tss/2
pvalue 3 1 bptest
(*  create square and cross product terms  *)
square -o intrate gnp ;
(*  estimate auxiliary regression for the White's test  *)
ols usq 0 intrate gnp sq_intra sq_gnp int_gnp ;
(*  compute TRsquare statistic and its p-value  *)
```

77

```
genr trsq=$nobs*$rsq
pvalue 3 5 trsq
```

The output can be obtained with the command

ecslib data4-11 < ex8-5.inp > ex8-5.out

Goldfeld-Quandt test: The first 8 and the last 8 observations were used in the estimation (the middle 7 were excluded). Regress housing against a constant, interest rate, and GNP. The F-statistic is $F_c = \hat{\sigma}_1^2 / \hat{\sigma}_2^2 = 17815 / 17415 = 1.02$, which is insignificant even at the 25 percent level. Thus there is no evidence of heteroscedasticity.

Breusch-Pagan test: The first step is to regress housing against a constant, interest rate, and GNP, using all 23 observations. Next, square the residuals and obtain $Z_t = \hat{u}_t^2 / \hat{\sigma}^2$, where $\hat{\sigma}^2 = (\Sigma \hat{u}_t^2)/T$ is an estimate of the error variance (σ^2). Suppose population has caused the heteroscedasticity and the error variance is $\sigma_t^2 = \alpha_0 + \alpha_1 POP_t^2 + v_t$. The null hypothesis is $\alpha_1 = 0$. To test this, regress Z_t against a constant and the square of population. Let RSS be the regression sum of squared from this auxiliary regression. The test statistic RSS/2 has a χ_1^2 distribution under the null hypothesis. In our example $RSS/2 = 1.199$, which is also insignificant at the 25 percent level.

White's test: Here also the first step is to estimate the basic model and obtain $\hat{u}_t^2$. Then regress $\hat{u}_t^2$ against a constant, INTRATE, GNP, INTRATE^2, GNP^2, and INTRATE $\times$ GNP. TR^2 from this auxiliary regression is χ_5^2 under the null hypothesis of homoscedasticity. In our example, $TR^2 = 5.06$. This too is insignificant at the 25 percent level.

Thus all three tests yield the same conclusion, namely, that there is no evidence of heteroscedasticity. Suppose heteroscedasticity had been significant. Then the WLS procedure is to estimate $\hat{\sigma}_t^2$ from the auxiliary regression in the White test and then set $w_t = 1/\hat{\sigma}_t$. If any of the $\hat{\sigma}_t^2$ values is not positive, $\ln(\hat{u}_t^2)$ would be used in the auxiliary regression and $\hat{\sigma}_t^2$ predicted from that.

EX 8.6

The following *ECSLIB* commands will be useful in estimating the model, using the data file *DATA8-1*.

```
ols exptrav 0 income ;
genr lnusq = log (uhat*uhat)
genr incmsq = income*income
ols lnusq 0 income incmsq ;
genr usqhat = exp(lnusq-uhat)
genr wt = 1/(usqhat ^ 0.5)
wls wt exptrav 0 income ;
```

The WLS estimated model is given by

$$\widehat{EXPTRAV} = 0.66803 + 0.0629 INCOME$$
$$(2.23) \quad (9.37)$$

The *t*-value of the regression coefficient for INCOME is lower than that for the WLS estimate in Table 8.2. Thus, using the logarithm of $\hat{u}_t^2$ as the dependent variable is not helpful in this example.

EX 8.7

In Table 4.7 Model C would be judged as the "best" in terms of the selection criteria. The first step is to regress POVRATE against a constant, URB, EDUC2, EDUC3, UNEMP, and MEDINC, and save $\hat{u}_t^2$. Next obtain the squares and cross products of the above independent variables. Then regress $\hat{u}_t^2$ against the variables in the basic model plus these square and crossproduct terms. TR^2 from this auxiliary regression is the test statistic. Reject H_0 if TR^2 exceeds the critical χ^2. The following *ECSLIB* commands (and the data file *DATA4-13*)will be useful in performing the White's test.

```
(* EX 8.7, using DATA4-13, for Exercise 8.7 *)
ols povrate 0 urb educ2 educ3 unemp medinc;
genr usq = uhat*uhat
(* generate square and cross product terms *)
square -o urb educ2 educ3 unemp medinc ;
```

```
ols usq 0 urb educ2 educ3 unemp medinc 10 11 12 13 14 15 16 17 18
   19 20 21 22 23 24 ;
genr trsq = $nobs*$rsq
pvalue 3 15 trsq
```

In our example, $TR^2 = 20.151$ which is χ^2_{15} under the null hypothesis of homoscedasticity. The p-value for this is 0.166 which means that there is no evidence of heteroscedasticity. There is, therefore, no need to use WLS.

EX 8.8

The final model is $PRICE = \beta_1 + \beta_2\ SQFT + \beta_3\ YARD + ... + u$.

Goldfeld-Quandt test: First rearrange the observations according to increasing SQFT. Next use the first 20 and the last 20 observations to estimate the above model and compute $F_c = \hat{\sigma}^2_2 / \hat{\sigma}^2_1$. Under the null hypothesis, this is $F_{10,10}$. Reject H_0 if $F_c > F^*$, the point on $F_{10,10}$ such that the area to the right is equal to the level of significance.

Breusch-Pagan test: First estimate the above model and save $\hat{u}^2_t$. The auxiliary equation is $\sigma^2_t = \alpha_0 + \alpha_1\ SQFT^2_t + v_t$. Regress $\hat{u}^2_t / \hat{\sigma}^2$ against a constant and $SQFT^2_t$. One-half of the regression sum of squares (RSS) of this auxiliary regression is χ^2_1. Reject H_0 if $RSS/2$ exceeds χ^{2*}_1, where χ^{2*}_1 is the point on χ^2_1 to the right of which the area is the level of significance.

White's test: The auxiliary regression here is $\hat{u}^2_t$ against a constant and $SQFT^2_t$. TR^2 from this regression is the test statistic. Reject H_0 if $TR^2 > \chi^{2*}_1$.

If significant heteroscedasticity is ignored, estimates will be unbiased and consistent, but inefficient. WLS procedure will give more efficient estimates than OLS. The procedure is to predict $\hat{\sigma}^2_t$ from the auxiliary regression as $\hat{\sigma}^2_t = \hat{\alpha}_0 + \hat{\alpha}_1\ SQFT^2_t$. If any of these values is nonpositive, use $\ln(\hat{u}^2_t)$ and the dependent variable and estimate $\hat{\sigma}^2_t$ as $exp(\hat{\alpha}_0 + \hat{\alpha}_1\ SQFT^2_t)$, where exp is the exponential function. Next construct $w_t = 1/\hat{\sigma}_t$. Multiply every variable in the model, including the dependent variable and the constant term, by w_t and use these in estimation.

EX 8.9

Exercise 6.11 was open-ended in which the reader was asked to estimate several models. Because the final model is unknown, we only give a general procedure here. First estimate the "final" model and save $\hat{u}_t^2$. Next generate new variables which are squares and crossproducts of the independent variables of this model (*caution*: do not square the variable COAST because it is a dummy variable). Then regress $\hat{u}_t^2$ against the variables in the basic model plus the squares and crossproducts. Then perform a TR^2 test similar to the one in Exercise 8.7. The estimation procedure parallels that in the application in Section 8.3.

EX 8.10

In Table 6.8 Model C has the lowest values for the selection statistics and is used as the basic model here. Let $\hat{u}_t^2$ be the squares of the residuals from this model. White's test requires the squares and cross-products of all the independent variables. Note from the data in Table 6.9 that several variables are binary. Hence the square is the same and should not be used. Furthermore, the numerous squares and cross-products cause near multicollinearity and therefore the auxiliary regression is not estimable in this complete form. To avoid this problem, only the squares of WEIGHT, WBASE, and HEIGHT are used in the auxiliary regression. The following *ECSLIB* commands will be useful in performing the White's test.

```
ols 1 0 2 3 6 8 9 10 11 ;
genr usq = uhat * uhat
square 2 3 6 ;
ols usq 0 2 3 6 8 9 10 11 17 18 19 ;
genr trsq = $nobs*$rsq
genr usqhat = usq - uhat
print trsq usqhat ;
```

TR^2 for the auxiliary regression is 50.789 which is χ_3^2 and is extremely significant. We therefore conclude that there is significant heteroscedasticity, calling for a WLS procedure. If the auxiliary regression is used to predict σ_t^2, we note several negative values which are unacceptable. We therefore use the modified approach in which $\ln(\hat{u}_t^2)$ is used as the dependent variable in the auxiliary regression. Additional *ECSLIB* commands for this are listed below.

```
genr lnusq = log(usq)
ols lnusq 0 2 3 6 8 9 10 11 17 18 19 ;
genr usqhat = exp(lnusq-uhat)
genr wt = 1/(usqhat ^ 0.5)
wls wt 1 0 2 3 6 8 9 10 11 ;
```

WLS estimates of Model C in Table 8 are given below.

$$\widehat{PRICE} = 18.490 + 0.269\,WEIGHT - 0.087\,WBASE$$
$$\phantom{\widehat{PRICE} = }(5.1) \quad\;\; (7.1) \qquad\qquad (-2.8)$$

$$-0.165\,HEIGHT - 0.669\,CARB + 1.366\,TRANS$$
$$\;\;(-2.6) \qquad\qquad (-5.1) \qquad\quad (9.1)$$

$$+ 5.473\,CRUZ + 2.972\,TILT$$
$$\;\;(6.7) \qquad\quad (2.2)$$

These estimates are more efficient than those in Table 6.8 (except for *HEIGHT* and *TILT*).

82

CHAPTER 9

PRACTICE PROBLEMS

PP 9.1

The equation for the residuals is $u_t = \rho u_{t-1} + \varepsilon_t$. The null and alternative hypotheses are $\rho = 0$ and $\rho > 0$. The test would reject the null hypothesis if the Durbin-Watson statistic d is lower than d_L, where the latter is obtained from Appendix Table 5.5b. Practice Computer Session 5.1 has the necessary statistics for this test. The following table presents the Durbin-Watson statistics, the associated bounds (for a one-sided test), and the decision rule.

Model	k'	DW d	d_L	d_U	Decision
A	2	0.846	1.17	1.54	Reject
B	2	0.832	1.17	1.54	Reject
C	3	0.831	1.08	1.66	Reject

We note that the null hypothesis of no autocorrelation is rejected for all three models. This means that OLS estimates are inefficient, although unbiased and consistent.

PP 9.2

The following ECSLIB commands will be useful in obtaining the necessary test statistic for Model A of Example 5.1. The commands are similar for the other two models.

```
(*  PP 9.2, using DATA4-11, for Practice Problem 9.2  *)
ols housing 0 intrate pop ;
(*  save residuals for Model A above  *)
genr ua = uhat
(*  obtain u(t-1)  *)
```

```
genr ua1 = ua(-1)
(*  suppress the first observation for 1963  *)
smpl 1964 ;
(*  auxiliary regression for Model A *)
ols ua 0 ua1 intrate pop;
(*  compute TRsquare and p-value  *)
genr trsq = $nobs*$rsq
pvalue 3 1 trsq
```

The TR^2 statistic and the corresponding p-value for the three models are in the following table.

Model	TR^2	$p-value$
A	7.018	0.008
B	7.261	0.007
C	7.266	0.007

The low p-values reinforce the conclusion of Practice Problem 9.1, namely, there is strong serial correlation among the residuals of the models.

PP 9.3

The file DATA9-2 and the following ECSLIB commands will generate the information needed to answer this question.

```
(*  PP9.3, using DATA9-2, for Practice Problem  *)
logs 1 2 3 4 ;
ols 5 0 6 7 8 ;
corc 5 0 6 7 8 ;
hilu 5 0 6 7 8 ;
```

For that data, $T = 30$, $k' = 3$, $d = 0.981$, $d_L = 1.21$, and $d_U = 1.65$. Because $d < d_L$, there is evidence of serial correlation. The appropriate estimation procedure is either HILU or CORC. We note that these two procedures give estimates which are quite close.

EXERCISES

EX 9.2

To obtain the empirical results for this exercise create a text file called *ex9-2.inp* that contains the following ECSLIB commands.

```
(*  EX 9.2, using DATA4-11, for Exercise 9.2  *)
genr lph = log(housing/pop)
genr lpcgnp = log(gnp/pop)
genr lr = log(intrate)
(*  estimate model by OLS procedure  *)
ols lph 0 lpcgnp lr ;
(*  LM test for AR(1)  *)
genr ut = uhat
genr ut1 = ut(-1)
smpl 1964 ;
ols ut 0 ut1 lpcgnp lr ;
genr trsq1 = $nobs*$rsq
pvalue 3 1 trsq1
(*  reset sample range to the beginning and estimate by hilu-corc  *)
smpl 1963 ;
hilu lph 0 lpcgnp lr;
(*  LM test for AR(3)  *)
genr ut2 = ut(-2)
genr ut3 = ut(-3)
smpl 1966 ;
ols ut 0 ut1 ut2 ut3 lpcgnp lr ;
genr trsq3 = $nobs*$rsq
pvalue 3 3 trsq3
smpl 1963 ;
(*  estimate model by AR procedure  *)
ar 1 2 3 ; lph 0 lpcgnp lr ;
ar 1 2 ; lph 0 lpcgnp lr ;
```

Next execute the program with the command

85

ecslib data4-11 < ex9-2.inp > ex9-2.out

and study the output file *ex9-2.out*.

We have, $T = 23$, $k' = 2$, Durbin-Watson statistic $d = 0.808$, and $d_L = 1.17$. Because $d < d_L$, we conclude that there is significant first-order serial correlation. For the LM test, $TR^2 = 7.617$ and the corresponding *p*-value is 0.0058, which is extremely low. The LM test thus confirms the DW-test. Because serial correlation is present, OLS estimates are inefficient although unbiased and consistent.

When the model was estimated by the mixed HILU-CORC procedure, DW *d* was 1.002 which suggests that autocorrelation persists. An LM test for AR(3) was next performed. TR^2 for this is 14.295 with a *p*-value 0.0025 which is considerably small suggesting support for the hypothesis that the residuals follow an AR(3) process. The model was then reestimated by the AR procedure and it was found that the AR(3) term is very insignificant. AR(2) was next applied and the estimated values and associated statistics are given below.

VARIABLE	COEFFICIENT	STDERROR	T STAT	PROB t > |T|
constant	-3.53350	1.14462	-3.087	0.0064 ***
lpcgnp	3.69482	0.61184	6.039	< 0.0001 ***
lr	-1.76622	0.23275	-7.588	< 0.0001 ***
ESTIMATES OF THE AR COEFFICIENTS				
ut_1	1.20872	0.13601	8.887	< 0.0001 ***
ut_2	-0.77819	0.12403	-6.274	< 0.0001 ***

Adjusted R-squared (computed as the square of the corr. between observed and predicted dep. var.) is 0.909.

The model explains 90.9 percent of the variation in the logarithm of per capita housing starts and all the coefficients are significant at levels below 0.01 percent. As expected, the interest rate elasticity is negative. The income elasticity is extremely high indicating that a one percent increase in per capita income is expected to increase per capita housing demand by 3.7 percent. Demand is also elastic with respect to the interest rate but the numerical value is much lower. The model might suffer from the "omitted variable bias", however, because there is no price index of housing included in the model.

EX 9.3

We have $T = 27$, $k' = 2$, $d = 0.65$, $d_L = 1.24$, and $d_U = 1.56$. Because $d < d_L$, a significant first-order autocorrelation is indicated. By Property 9.1, estimates and forecasts are unbiased and consistent, but inefficient. Tests of hypotheses are invalid and the goodness of fit is generally exaggerated. A procedure that gives more efficient estimates is the CORC procedure; (1) regress LH against a constant, LY, and LP, and save $\hat{u}_t$, (2) compute $\hat{\rho}$ from equation (9.7), (3) obtain $LH_t^* = LH_t - \hat{\rho} LH_{t-1}$, $LY_t^* = LY_t - \hat{\rho} LY_{t-1}$, and $LP_t^* = LP_t - \hat{\rho} LP_{t-1}$, (4) regress LH_t^* against a constant, LY_t^*, and LP_t^* and obtain the parameter estimates and a new $\hat{u}_t$, (5) go back to step (2) and iterate until two successive $\hat{\rho}$ values do not differ much.

EX 9.5

We have, $T = 32$, $k' = 1$, $d = 0.207$, $d_L = 1.37$, and $d_U = 1.50$. Let the error term be $u_t = \rho u_{t-1} + \varepsilon_t$ where ε_t is "well-behaved." The null hypothesis is $\rho = 0$ and the alternative is $\rho > 0$. Because $d < d_L$ we reject the null hypothesis and conclude that there is significant first-order autocorrelation. We are not justified in feeling that the fit is excellent and that the coefficients are highly significant. This is because serial correlation makes the tests invalid and the goodness of fit is generally exaggerated.

EX 9.6

For this model $T = 60$, $k' = 3$, $d = 0.53$, $d_L = 1.48$, and $d_U = 1.69$. Because $d < d_L$, we infer that there is significant first-order autocorrelation. Therefore, t-tests are invalid and R^2 is generally an overestimate of the true value. The statements are therefore correct.

EX 9.7

The following *ECSLIB* commands will be useful in obtaining the output needed to answer the questions here (use the data file *DATA9-11*).

```
(* EX 9.7, using DATA9-11, for Exercise 9.7 *)
ols profits 0 sales;
(* LM test for first-order serial correlation *)
genr ut=uhat
genr time
graph ut time;
genr ut1 = ut(-1)
smpl 1951 ;
ols ut 0 sales ut1;
genr trsq1 = $nobs*$rsq
pvalue 3 1 trsq1
smpl 1950 ;
corc profits 0 sales;
hilu profits 0 sales;
(* LM test for higher order serial correlation *)
genr ut2 = ut(-2)
genr ut3 = ut(-3)
smpl 1953 ;
ols ut 0 ut1 ut2 ut3 sales ;
genr trsq3 = $nobs*$rsq
pvalue 3 3 trsq3
ar 1 2 3 ; profits 0 sales ;
ar 1 2 ; profits 0 sales ;
```

The residual plot exhibits a clustering effect indicating serial correlation. $T = 39$, $k' = 1$, $d = 0.955$, and $d_L = 1.43$. There is evidence of serial correlation $(d < d_L)$ here. For the LM test, regress $\hat{u}_t$ against a constant, sales, and $\hat{u}_{t-1}$. For this auxiliary regression $TR^2 = 7.798$ with a p-value of 0.0052. Such a low value strongly rejects the null hypothesis of no first order serial correlation. The estimates using CORC and the mixed HILU-CORC are not very close. The DW statistic for the residuals of the transformed model is 1.2, which is insignificant. A test for higher order serial correlation is therefore indicated. TR^2 for AR(3) is 10.767 with a p-value of 0.013, which makes AR(3) significant. The model was then reestimated by the AR procedure and it was found that the AR(3) term is very insignificant. AR(2) was next applied and the estimated values and associated statistics are given below.

VARIABLE	COEFFICIENT	STDERROR	T STAT	PROB t > |T|
constant	-0.38494	4.22564	-0.091	0.9280
sales	0.04808	0.00313	15.355	< 0.0001 ***
ESTIMATES OF THE AR COEFFICIENTS				
ut_1	0.78118	0.20002	3.905	0.0005 ***
ut_2	-0.40772	0.20008	-2.038	0.0499 **

Adjusted R-squared computed as the square of the corr. between observed and predicted dep. var. is 0.944.

Both the AR terms are significant at the 5 percent level and the sales coefficient is significant at the 1 percent level. The model explains 94.4 percent of the variation in profits. A one thousand dollar increase in sales is expected to increase the profits, on average, by $48.08.

EX 9.8
The data file *DATA9-2* and the following *ECSLIB* commands will be helpful in estimating this model.

```
(*  EX 9-8.inp, using DATA9-2, for Exercise 9.8  *)
logs demand income price temp;
ols l_demand 0 l_income l_price l_temp;
genr ut=uhat
lags ut;
print ut ut_1;
corc l_demand 0 l_income l_price l_temp;
hilu l_demand 0 l_income l_price l_temp;
smpl 2;
ols ut 0 l_income l_price l_temp ut_1;
genr trsq = $nobs*$rsq
pvalue 3 1 trsq
```

(a) The error term is assumed to be $u_t = \rho u_{t-1} + \varepsilon_t$, the null hypothesis is $\rho = 0$, and the alternative is $\rho > 0$. For the DW test, $d = 0.981$, $T = 30$, $k' = 3$, $d_L = 1.21$, and $d_U = 1.65$. There is evidence of first-order auto-correlation because $d < d_L$. For the LM test, estimate the model and obtain $\hat{u}_t$. Then regress $\hat{u}_t$ against a constant, l_price, l_income, l_temp, and $\hat{u}_{t-1}$. $(T-1)R^2 = 6.098$. Because the corresponding p-value is 0.014, we reject the null hypothesis (at 1.4 percent) and conclude that there is significant autocorrelation.

(b) By Property 9.1, estimates are unbiased and consistent but inefficient.

(c) *HILU procedure*: First generate $l\_demand_t^* = l\_demand_t - \hat{\rho}$ l_demand_{t-1} (where $\hat{\rho}$ is any value between -1 and +1) and similarly for the other variables. Use these transformed variables and estimate the modified model and compute its error sum of squares (ESS). Next choose a different $\hat{\rho}$ and repeat the procedure. By systematically search-ing from -1 to +1, we get a series of ESS values. Choose that $\hat{\rho}$ for which ESS is the lowest. The estimates corresponding to these are the HILU estimates. Estimates are "better" in the sense of greater asymp-totic efficiency.

EX 9.9

(a) The following *ECSLIB* commands and the data set *DATA9-12* will be useful in obtaining the information needed to answer this question.

```
(*  EX 9.9, using DATA9-12, for Exercise 9.9  *)
logs QNC PRICE INCOME PRIME STOCK UNEMP;
corr l_PRICE l_INCOME l_PRIME l_UNEMP
 STRIKE SPRING ;
ols l_QNC 0 l_PRICE l_INCOME l_PRIME l_UNEMP
 STRIKE SPRING;
genr ut = uhat
lags ut ;
smpl 1970.2 ;
```

90

```
ols ut 0 ut_1 1_PRICE 1_INCOME 1_PRIME 1_UNEMP
STRIKE SPRING;
genr trsq1 = $nobs*$rsq
pvalue 3 1 trsq1
(* LM test for fourth-order serial correlation *)
smpl 1971.1 ;
ols ut 0 ut_1 ut_2 ut_3 ut_4 1_PRICE 1_INCOME
1_PRIME 1_UNEMP STRIKE SPRING;
genr trsq4 = $nobs*$rsq
pvalue 3 1 trsq4
(* estimation by the AR procedure *)
ar 1 2 3 4 ; 1_QNC 0 1_PRICE 1_INCOME 1_PRIME
1_UNEMP STRIKE SPRING;
ar 1 2 3 4 ; 1_QNC 0 1_INCOME 1_PRIME 1_UNEMP
SPRING;
smpl 1970.4 ;
ar 1 2 3 ; 1_QNC 0 1_INCOME 1_PRIME 1_UNEMP
SPRING;
```

(b) Multicollinearity does not appear to be a problem in this data set because most of the correlation coefficients are low.

(c) For the auxiliary regression, $(T-1)R^2 = 1.884$ and its p-value is 0.17 which is unacceptably high. Thus there is no evidence of first-order serial correlation. The estimates are therefore unbiased, consistent, and BLUE. Standard errors are also consistent and tests of hypotheses are valid.

(d) Because there is no first-order serial correlation, no modification is necessary.

(e) Estimate the auxiliary regression with $\hat{u}_t$ as the dependent variable and the added independent variables, $\hat{u}_{t-1}$, $\hat{u}_{t-2}$, $\hat{u}_{t-3}$, and $\hat{u}_{t-4}$. Here $(T-4)R^2 = 7.837$ and p-value = 0.005. Higher order serial correlation is indicated at the 0.5 percent level. Autocorrelation of order 4 is therefore suggested with the residual equation $u_t = \rho_1 u_{t-1} + \rho_2 u_{t-2} + \rho_3 u_{t-3} + \rho_4 u_{t-4} + \varepsilon_t$. The appropriate estimation procedure is the generalized CORC method described in Section 9.5. The results indicate that all the elasticities are significantly different from zero with the exception of the price elasticity. Autocorrelation coefficients are also significant except for the AR(1) term (see the ECSLIB output corresponding to this exercise for additional analysis). Estimates and test statistics are asymptotically more efficient because serial correlation is explicitly taken care of.

EX 9.10

(a) To obtain the empirical results needed to answer this question, use the data file *DATA9-13* and the following *ECSLIB* commands.

```
(*  EX 9.10, using DATA9-13, for Exercise 9.10  *)
corr Mt Gt Tt Xt;
ols Yt 0 Mt Gt Tt Xt;
(*  LM test for first-order autocorrelation  *)
genr ut=uhat
lags ut;
smpl 1959.2 ;
ols ut 0 ut_1 Mt Gt Tt Xt ;
genr trsq1 = $nobs*$rsq
pvalue 3 1 trsq1
(*  estimate by CORC procedure  *)
smpl 1959.1 ;
corc Yt 0 Mt Gt Tt Xt;
(*  LM test for fourth-order autocorrelation  *)
smpl 1960.1 ;
ols ut 0 ut_1 ut_2 ut_3 ut_4 Mt Gt Tt Xt;
genr trsq4 = $nobs*$rsq
pvalue 3 4 trsq4
(*  estimate model by the AR procedure  *)
smpl 1959.1;
ar 1 2 3 4 ; Yt 0 Mt Gt Tt Xt;
ar 1 3 4 ; Yt 0 Mt Gt Tt Xt;
```

(* the following model indicates that AR(1) is a better specification *)
ar 1 3 ; Yt 0 Mt Gt Tt Xt;
hilu Yt 0 Mt Gt Tt Xt;

(b) An increase in money supply, government expenditure, or exports is likely to be expansionary and hence we would expect positive signs for these coefficients. Taxes are contractionary and hence we would expect a negative sign. The signs for the coefficients of G_t and T_t are counter-intuitive. A strong possible reason for this opposite result is the near perfect correlation among the dependent variables. All the pairwise correlation coefficients are at least 0.96. This strong multicollinearity can reverse signs, as was illustrated in Example 5.2.

(c) For the DW test, $T = 104$, $k' = 4$, $d = 0.401$, $d_L = 1.59$, and $d_U = 1.76$ (the entry for $T = 100$ is used here). Because $d < d_L$ we conclude that there is significant first-order serial correlation. For the LM test, $(T - 1)R^2 = 68.909$ and p-value is below 0.00001. Therefore both tests indicate strong first-order autocorrelation. By Property 9.1, estimates are unbiased and consistent but not efficient.

(d) First estimate the model by OLS and get $\hat{u}_t$. Next compute $\hat{\rho}$ using equation (9.7). Then transform the variables; $Y_t^* = Y_t - \hat{\rho} Y_{t-1}, M_t^* = M_t - \hat{\rho} M_{t-1}$, and so on. Next regress Y_t^* against a constant, M_t^*, G_t^*, and so on. From these obtain new estimates of $\hat{u}_t$ and $\hat{\rho}$. Iterate this procedure until two successive values of $\hat{\rho}$ do not differ by more than a small amount (say 0.01). Estimates obtained this way are "improved" because they are asymptotically more efficient than OLS estimates.

(e) The auxiliary regression for the LM test for fourth-order autocorrelation is to regress $\hat{u}_t$ against a constant, $Mt, Gt, Tt, Xt, \hat{u}_{t-1}, \hat{u}_{t-2}, \hat{u}_{t-3}$, and $\hat{u}_{t-4}$. $(T-4)R^2 = 68.302$ and p-value is below 0.0001 which is extremely significant. The generalized CORC procedure indicates that some of the $\hat{u}_{t-i}$ terms are very insignificant. When these were eliminated one at a time, we find that AR(1) is appropriate. The model was

93

therefore estimated by the mixed HILU-CORC procedure. Because serial correlation is explicitly taken care of, estimates are asymptotically more efficient than OLS estimates. We note that the coefficient for G_t has the expected positive sign but it is not significant. The sign for T_t is still positive.

EX 9.11

The basic model is $E_t = \alpha + \beta T_t + u_t$. To allow for the summer and winter differential, one would obtain quarterly data and define seasonal dummies, SUMMER, WINTER, and SPRING which take the value 1 in the corresponding quarter and 0 during other quarters. The control season is the fall. To allow for differential temperature effects for low, medium, and high temperatures, we use the piece-wise linear regression approach described in Section 6.3. Let D4560 = 1 if temperature is between 45 and 60 degrees, D6070 = 1 if temperature is between 60 and 70 degrees, and D70 = 1 when temperature is above 70 degrees. The following formulation is piece-wise linear [refer to equation (6.24)] in which the t subscript has been omitted for convenience.

$$E = a + bT + c\,D4560(T-45) + d\,D6070(T-60) + e\,D70(T-70) + u$$

Now we have to allow the regression coefficients to be different across the seasons. For example, let $a = a_0 + a_1 SUMMER + a_2 WINTER + a_3 SPRING$, and so on for the others. The completely general model is as follows.

$$
\begin{aligned}
E = {}& a_0 + a_1 SUMMER + a_2 WINTER + a_3 SPRING \\
& + T(b_0 + b_1 SUMMER + b_2 WINTER + b_3 SPRING) \\
& + D4560(T-45)(c_0 + c_1 SUMMER + c_2 WINTER \\
& + c_3 SPRING) + D6070(T-60)(d_0 + d_1 SUMMER \\
& + d_2 WINTER + d_3 SPRING) + D70(T-70)(e_0 + e_1 SUMMER \\
& + e_2 WINTER + e_3 SPRING) + u
\end{aligned}
$$

To obtain a conclusive result for a test on serial correlation, we need to use the LM test. First estimate the above model and save the residuals $\hat{u}_t$. Next regress $\hat{u}_t$ against $\hat{u}_{t-1}$ and all the other variables in the above model. The statistic $(T-1)R^2$ has the Chi-square distribution with d.f. 1 under the null hypothesis of no serial correlation. If the *p*-value is below some level, we would reject the null hypothesis and conclude that there is significant auto-correlation. If this is the case, then we would use the mixed HILU-CORC procedure described in Section 9.4 in order to obtain estimates that are more efficient than OLS estimates.

EX 9.12
The relevant data file for this is *DATA9-14*. First create the text file *ex9-12.inp* with following ECSLIB commands.

```
(* EX 9.12, using DATA9-14, for Exercise 9.12 *)
genr y = rpm/pop
genr price = oprev/rpm
genr pcgnp = gnp/pop
genr accpm = accid/rpm
logs y price pcgnp accpm  ;
(* estimate double-log model *)
ols l_y const regu l_price l_pcgnp l_accpm fatal  ;
(* save residuals and generate their lags *)
genr ut = uhat
genr ut1 = ut(-1)
genr ut2 = ut(-2)
genr ut3 = ut(-3)
(* LM test for first-order serial correlation *)
smpl 1948 ;
ols ut const ut1 regu l_price l_pcgnp l_accpm fatal  ;
genr trsq1 = $nobs*$rsq
pvalue 3 1 trsq1
(* LM test for third-order serial correlation *)
smpl 1950 ;
ols ut const ut1 ut2 ut3 regu l_price l_pcgnp l_accpm fatal  ;
genr trsq2 = $nobs*$rsq
pvalue 3 3 trsq2
smpl 1947 ;
```

```
(* estimate model by HILU and CORC procedures *)
corc l_y const regu l_price l_pcgnp l_accpm fatal ;
hilu l_y const regu l_price l_pcgnp l_accpm fatal ;
(* test whether elasticities depend on regulation *)
genr rl_price = regu*l_price
genr rl_pcgnp = regu*l_pcgnp
genr rl_accpm = regu*l_accpm
genr rfatal = regu*fatal
ols l_y const regu l_price rl_price l_pcgnp rl_pcgnp l_accpm rl_accpm
 fatal ;
genr utt = uhat
genr utt1 = utt(-1)
genr utt2 = utt(-2)
genr utt3 = utt(-3)
smpl 1950 ;
ols utt const utt1 utt2 utt3 regu l_price rl_price l_pcgnp rl_pcgnp
 l_accpm rl_accpm fatal ;
genr trsq3 = $nobs*$rsq
pvalue 3 3 trsq3
(* reset sample range to the beginning and use AR to estimate model *)
smpl 1947 ;
ar 1 2 3 ;
l_y const regu l_price rl_price l_pcgnp rl_pcgnp l_accpm rl_accpm
 fatal ;
(* omit insignificant variables a few at a time *)
omit l_accpm ;
omit rl_accpm ;
omit rl_pcgnp ;
omit regu ;
omit fatal ;
```

Next execute the program with the command

```
ecslib -v50 data9-14 < ex9-12.inp > ex9-12.out
```

The flag -*v*50 is needed to override the default limit set for the number of variables. [The execution might take 10 to 15 minutes].

The Durbin-Watson $d = 0.796$, $T = 41$, $k' = 5$, $d_L = 1.23$, and $D_U = 1.79$. Because $d < d_L$, we reject the null hypothesis of no serial correlation and conclude that it is significant. This means that OLS estimates, though unbiased and consistent, are inefficient. For the LM test, $TR^2 = 19.18$ with a p-value of 0.000012 which is extremely low. This test also rejects the null hypothesis. CORC and HILU procedures yield estimates which are very close to each other.

To test for structural change, first create the three new variables *rl_price*, *rl_pcgnp*, and *rl_accpm* which are defined above as the products of the regulation dummy variable and corresponding independent variable. The model with complete interactions is given below.

$$l\_y = \alpha_0 + \alpha_1 regu + l\_price\,(\beta_0 + \beta_1 regu) + l\_pcgnp\,(\gamma_0 + \gamma_1 regu)$$
$$+ l\_accpm\,(\delta_0 + \delta_1 regu) + \varepsilon fatal + u_t$$

This model was tested for AR(3) which was found to be present. The Generalized CORC procedure was next estimated and insignificant terms omitted one at a time until a "final" model was obtained in which all regression coefficients were significant at the 10 percent level or at a lower level. The estimated final model is given in the next page. The model explaines 99.9 percent of the variation in the logarithm of per capita revenue passenger miles and all the AR coefficients are significant. However, the regulation and fatality variables are generally not significant. The only exception is the elasticity with respect to price. When regulation was in effect (regu = 0), the price elasticity was -0.619, whereas when it was lifted the elasticity decreased (in numerical terms) to -0.602. Thus, deregulation made price slightly less elastic.

97

VARIABLE	COEFFICIENT	STDERROR	T STAT	PROB t > |T|
constant	0.34977	0.41229	0.848	0.4022
l_price	-0.61868	0.08782	-7.045	< 0.0001 ***
rl_price	0.01689	0.00775	2.180	0.0363 **
l_pcgnp	0.97276	0.11759	8.273	< 0.0001 ***

ESTIMATES OF THE AR COEFFICIENTS

ut_1	0.95427	0.14911	6.400	< 0.0001 ***
ut_2	0.36794	0.18548	1.984	0.0552 *
ut_3	-0.37427	0.12261	-3.053	0.0043 ***

Adjusted R-squared computed as the square of the corr. between observed and
predicted dep. var. is 0.999.

EX 9.13

Use the following ECSLIB commands and the data file *DATA9-15* to generate
the output needed to answer this question.

```
(* EX 9.13, using DATA9-15, for Exercise 9.13 *)
logs 2 3 4 5 6 7 ;
ols 8 0 9 10 11 12 13 ;
(* save residuals, lag them, and do LM tests for AR 1 and 3 *)
genr ut = uhat
genr ut1 = ut(-1)
genr ut2 = ut(-2)
genr ut3 = ut(-3)
smpl 1949;
ols ut 0 ut1 9 10 11 12 13 ;
genr trsq1 = $nobs*$rsq
pvalue 3 1 trsq1
smpl 1951 ;
ols ut 0 ut1 ut2 ut3 9 10 11 12 13 ;
genr trsq3 = $nobs*$rsq
pvalue 3 3 trsq3
(* reset sample range to the beginning and use AR procedure *)
```

```
smpl 1948 ;
ar 1 2 3 ; 8 0 9 10 11 12 13 ;
corr 9 10 11 12 13 ;
```

TR^2 for first-order autocorrelation is 39.483 with a *p*-value below 0.00001. For the third-order, the test statistic is 37.718 and is highly significant suggesting an AR(3) error process. The Generalized CORC was applied and the results are as follows.

VARIABLE	COEFFICIENT	STDERROR	T STAT	PROB t > |T|
constant	10.32082	0.60572	17.039	< 0.0001 ***
l_labor	0.56439	0.07847	7.193	< 0.0001 ***
l_land	-0.98848	0.06485	-15.243	< 0.0001 ***
l_machin	0.60357	0.10233	5.898	< 0.0001 ***
l_fert	-0.86236	0.08410	-10.254	< 0.0001 ***
l_seedfe	-0.39955	0.09101	-4.390	0.0001 ***
ESTIMATES OF THE AR COEFFICIENTS				
ut_1	-1.02628	0.07327	-14.007	< 0.0001 ***
ut_2	0.39109	0.13206	2.962	0.0055 ***
ut_3	0.76990	0.07375	10.440	< 0.0001 ***

Adjusted R-squared computed as the square of the corr. between observed and predicted dep. var. is 0.996.

The model explains 99.6 percent of the logarithm of the agricultural output index and all the regression and AR coefficients are significant at the 1 percent level. However, several coefficients have negative elasticities which are counterintuitive. A possible explanation is multicollinearity among the explanatory variables. Although pair-wise correlations are not very high, it is possible that several independent variables are jointly collinear.

EX 9.14

First create an ECSLIB command input file called *ex9-14.inp* containing the following lines.

```
(*  EX 9.14, using DATA6-13, for Exercise 9.14  *)
genr dummy
(* reset sample range to the first period only *)
smpl 1983.01 1986.06
(* Next estimate Model C *)
ols Q const P HS SHC OC dummy_2 dummy_3 dummy_4 dummy_5
 dummy_6 dummy_7 dummy_8 dummy_9 dummy_10 dummy_11
 dummy_12 ;
(*  LM test for 12-th order serial correlation  *)
genr ut = uhat
lags ut ;
smpl 1984.01 ;
ols ut const P HS SHC OC dummy_2 dummy_3 dummy_4 dummy_5
 dummy_6 dummy_7 dummy_8 dummy_9 dummy_10 dummy_11
 dummy_12 ut_1 ut_2 ut_3 ut_4 ut_5 ut_6 ut_7 ut_8 ut_9
 ut_10 ut_11 ut_12 ;
genr trsq = $nobs*$rsq
pvalue 3 12 trsq
(*  reset sample range to the beginning and use AR procedure  *)
smpl 1983.01 ;
ar 1 2 3 4 5 6 7 8 9 10 11 12 ; Q const P HS SHC OC dummy_2
 dummy_3 dummy_4 dummy_5 dummy_6 dummy_7 dummy_8
 dummy_9 dummy_10 dummy_11 dummy_12 ;
ar 1 2 3 5 7 8 9 10 11 12 ; Q const P HS SHC OC dummy_2
 dummy_3 dummy_4 dummy_5 dummy_6 dummy_7 dummy_8
 dummy_9 dummy_10 dummy_11 dummy_12 ;
(* This is the final model with all significant coefficients *)
ar 1 2 3 5 7 8 9 10 11 12 ; Q const P HS SHC OC dummy_4
 dummy_5 dummy_6 dummy_7 dummy_8 dummy_9 dummy_10
 dummy_11 dummy_12 ;
(* obtain predicted values for the loss and post loss periods *)
fcast 1986.07 1990.05 Qhat ;
(* reset sample range to the second and third periods *)
smpl 1986.07 1990.05
(* compute loss in sales for each month *)
```

```
genr Qloss = Qhat - Q
(* compute loss in revenues for each month *)
genr dolrloss = P*Qloss
(* set sample range to the middle period *)
smpl 1986.07 1988.10
(* compute sum of losses during the litigation period *)
genr totqloss = 28*mean(Qloss)
genr totdloss = 28*mean(dolrloss)
(* print the values *)
smpl 1986.07 1986.07
print -o totqloss totdloss ;
(* reset sample range for the post loss period *)
smpl 1988.11 1990.05
(* compute sum of losses for this period *)
genr qloss2 = 19*mean(Qloss)
genr dloss2 = 19*mean(dolrloss)
(* print the values *)
smpl 1988.11 1988.11
print -o qloss2 dloss2  ;
```

Then execute these with the DOS command

$$\text{ecslib -v50 data6-13} < \text{ex9-14.inp} > \text{ex9-14.out}$$

and study the output file *ex9-14.out*. Because the variable list and the number of lags are long, the execution might take 20 to 30 minutes.

As in Section 6.8, the estimation was done using data for the first period, namely, 1983.01 through 1986.06, but using a general specification for the error structure. TR^2 statistic for 12-th order autocorrelation is 27.523 with a p-value of 0.0065 which suggests the strong presence of serial correlation. The model was therefore estimated by the Generalized CORC procedure with an AR(12) residual equation. It was found that lags 4 and were insignificant as were the dummy variables for February and March. These were then eliminated and the model estimated by the AR procedure. The final model was used to predict the loss in sales and revenues over the subsequent periods. The following table summarizes the loss in sales and revenues using both the OLS procedure applied in Chapter 6 and the AR procedure applied here.

Period	Sales loss		Revenue loss	
	OLS	AR	OLS	AR
1986.07 - 1988.10	54,209	62,730	481,575	501,511
1988.11 - 1990.05	38,467	36,166	335,597	312,813
Total	92,676	98,896	817,172	814,324

The sales loss is considerably higher when the AR estimates are used but the revenue loss is slightly less. Since the AR specification is econometrically better justified, the estimates one should go by are the ones presented here.

EX 9.15
First create a text file called *ex9-15.inp* with the following ECSLIB commands.

```
(* EX 9.15, using DATA9-16, for Exercise 9.15 *)
genr pcsales = numcars/pop
logs pcsales price income intrate unemp ;
(* Stage I *)
ols l_pcsale const l_price l_income l_intrat l_unemp ;
genr ut = uhat
genr ut1 = ut(-1)
smpl 1976.2 ;
(* auxiliary regression for AR(1) *)
ols ut 0 ut1 l_price l_income l_intrat l_unemp ;
genr trsq1 = $nobs*$rsq
pvalue 3 1 trsq1 ;
smpl 1976.1 ;
corc l_pcsale const l_price l_income l_intrat l_unemp ;
hilu l_pcsale const l_price l_income l_intrat l_unemp ;
```

```
hilu l_pcsale const l_price l_income l_intrat ;
(* Stage II, create seasonal dummies and test for seasonal effects *)
genr dummy
ols l_pcsale const dummy_2 dummy_3 dummy_4 l_price l_income
 l_intrat ;
genr utt = uhat
genr utt1 = utt(-1)
smpl 1976.2 ;
ols utt const utt1 dummy_2 dummy_3 dummy_4 l_price l_income
 l_intrat ;
genr trsq2 = $nobs*$rsq
pvalue 3 1 trsq2;
smpl 1976.1 ;
hilu l_pcsale const dummy_2 dummy_3 dummy_4 l_price l_income
 l_intrat ;
(* Stage III, higher order serial correlation *)
lags utt ;
smpl 1977.1 ;
ols utt const utt_1 utt_2 utt_3 utt_4 dummy_2 dummy_3 dummy_4
 l_price l_income l_intrat ;
genr trsq3 = $nobs*$rsq
pvalue 3 4 trsq3
smpl 1976.1 ;
ar 1 2 3 4 ; l_pcsale const dummy_2 dummy_3 dummy_4 l_price
 l_income l_intrat ;
ar 1 3 4 ; l_pcsale const dummy_2 dummy_3 dummy_4 l_price
 l_income l_intrat ;
ar 1 4 ; l_pcsale const dummy_2 dummy_3 dummy_4 l_price
 l_income l_intrat ;
ar 1 ; l_pcsale const dummy_2 dummy_3 dummy_4 l_price
 l_income l_intrat ;
omit dummy_4 ;
```

The output for this exercise can be obtained with the DOS command which might take 15 to 20 minutes to execute.

The model was first estimated by OLS and tests were performed for first-order serial correlation. TR^2 for the LM test was 3.247 with a p-value of 0.072. The CORC and HILU procedures gave extremely close results, but the unemployment coefficient was very insignificant and was omitted from further analysis. The LM test for including seasonal dummies gave a TR^2 of 5.324 with a corresponding p-value of 0.021 which indicates strong significance. LM test for AR(4) gave a $(T-4)R^2$ of 7.993 and the p-value 0.092 indicating weak significance. The AR procedure was next used, insignificant residual terms were eliminated, and the model reestimated. The final model was found to be AR(1) with the following estimates.

VARIABLE	COEFFICIENT	STDERROR	T STAT	PROB t > |T|	
constant	-33.73661	2.99175	-11.277	< 0.0001	***
dummy_2	0.12805	0.02740	4.674	< 0.0001	***
dummy_3	-0.04516	0.02734	-1.651	0.1082	
l_price	-1.75998	0.12253	-14.364	< 0.0001	***
l_income	4.94461	0.38060	12.991	< 0.0001	***
l_intrat	-0.20858	0.03129	-6.666	< 0.0001	***

Adjusted R-squared computed as the square of the corr. between observed and predicted dep. var. is 0.882.

The model explains 88.2 percent of the variation in the logarithm of per capita car sales. All the coefficients are significant, although the dummy variable for the third quarter is significant only at the 10.82 percent level. The coefficients have the expected signs, the price elasticity is -1.76, but the income elasticity is considerably higher (4.945). Per capita car sales is inelastic with respect to the interest rate (-0.209).

CHAPTER 10

PRACTICE PROBLEMS

PP 10.1
To get the long run multiplier set $Y_t = Y^*$ and $X_t = X^*$ for all t. $Y^* = \alpha + \beta_0 X^* + \beta_0 \lambda X^* + \ldots = \alpha + \beta_0 X^*(1 + \lambda + \lambda^2 + \ldots) = \alpha + [\beta_0 X^*/(1-\lambda)]$. The long-run multiplier is $\Delta Y^*/\Delta X^* = \beta_0/(1-\lambda)$.

PP 10.2
The relevant equations are obtained by setting $\alpha_3 = 0$ in the Almon lag equations. The model now becomes

$$Y_t = \alpha + \alpha_0(X_t + X_{t-1} + X_{t-2} + X_{t-3} + X_{t-4})$$
$$+ \alpha_1(X_{t-1} + 2X_{t-2} + 3X_{t-3} + 4X_{t-4})$$
$$+ \alpha_2(X_{t-1} + 4X_{t-2} + 9X_{t-3} + 16X_{t-4}) + u_t$$

The procedure is to generate the variables in parentheses and to use these as independent variables.

PP 10.3
We have $\beta_1 = 1 - \lambda$ and $\beta_2 = \beta\lambda$ from which we get $\hat{\lambda} = 1 - \hat{\beta}_1 = 1 - 0.667 = 0.333$, $\hat{\beta} = \hat{\beta}_2/\hat{\lambda} = 0.3/0.333 = 0.9$. The marginal effect of sales on desired inventories is $\hat{\beta} = 0.9$. The marginal effect on actual sales is $\hat{\beta}_2 = 0.3$. The average number of periods is $1/\hat{\lambda} = 3$.

PP 10.4
The impact multiplier is $\Delta Y_t/\Delta X_t = 0$ and the long-run multiplier is $\hat{\beta} = 0.9$. The interim multiplier for one period is $\Delta \hat{Y}_t/\Delta X_{t-1} = \hat{\beta}_2 = 0.3$. For two periods, $Y_t = \beta_0 + \beta_1(\beta_0 + \beta_1 Y_{t-2} + \beta_2 X_{t-2} + v_{t-1}) + \beta_2 X_{t-1} + v_t$. Hence $\Delta \hat{Y}_t/\Delta X_{t-2} = \hat{\beta}_1 \hat{\beta}_2 = 0.2$. For three periods, $\Delta \hat{Y}_t/\Delta X_{t-3} = \hat{\beta}_1^2 \hat{\beta}_2 = 0.133$, and for four periods it is $\hat{\beta}_1^3 \hat{\beta}_2 = 0.089$.

PP 10.5

If $u_t = (1-\lambda)u_{t-1} + \varepsilon_t$, from equation (10.16)

$$Y_t = \alpha\lambda + (1-\lambda)Y_{t-1} + \lambda\beta X_{t-1} + \varepsilon_t = \beta_0 + \beta_1 Y_{t-1} + \beta_2 X_{t-1} + \varepsilon_t$$

Because ε_t is well-behaved, OLS estimates of β_0, β_1, and β_2 are BLUE. Since $\lambda = 1-\beta$, the OLS estimate of λ is BLUE (Gauss-Markov Theorem) but $\hat{\alpha}$ and $\hat{\beta}$ are nonlinear functions of β_0, β_1, and β_2. The BLUE property does not extend to nonlinear functions.

EXERCISES

EX 10.2

(a)   Taking logarithms of the model we get

$$\ln Y_t = \alpha + \beta \ln X_t^* + u_t$$

Taking logarithms of the adaptive rule,

$$\ln X_t^* - \ln X_{t-1}^* = \gamma \ln X_{t-1} - \gamma \ln X_{t-1}^*$$

or

$$\ln X_t^* = \gamma \ln X_{t-1} + (1-\gamma) \ln X_{t-1}^*$$

From the model we have, $\ln X_t^* = (\ln Y_t - \alpha - u_t)/\beta$. Substituting this in the adaptive rule,

$$\frac{\ln Y_t - \alpha - u_t}{\beta} = \gamma \ln X_{t-1} + \frac{(1-\gamma)(\ln Y_{t-1} - \alpha - u_{t-1})}{\beta}$$

or

$$\ln Y_t = \alpha\gamma + (1-\gamma) \ln Y_{t-1} + \beta\gamma \ln X_{t-1} + u_t - (1-\gamma) u_{t-1}$$

$$= \beta_0 + \beta_1 \ln Y_{t-1} + \beta_2 \ln X_{t-1} + v_t$$

(b)   By Property 3.2, consistency requires that $E(v_t) = 0$, $E(v_t \ln Y_{t-1}) = 0$, and $E(v_t \ln X_{t-1}) = 0$.

(c) Because the model has a lagged dependent variable, OLS estimates are biased.

(d) If u_t is normally distributed with the specified properties, $\ln Y_{t-1}$ will be correlated with $u_t - (1-\gamma)u_{t-1}$ and hence Assumption 3.4 is violated. OLS estimates are therefore not consistent.

EX 10.3

(a) Even if there are no sales (that is, $S_t = 0$), inventories (α) will be positive. If sales increase, we would expect desired inventories to increase also, and hence β is likely to be positive. If desired inventories exceed actual inventories, we would expect actual inventories to increase and hence λ is likely to be positive. Also $\beta < 1$ and $\lambda < 1$, as otherwise the model will be explosive.

(b)

$$I_t = \lambda I_{t-1}^* + (1-\lambda)I_{t-1} + u_t = \lambda(\alpha+\beta S_{t-1}) + (1-\lambda)I_{t-1} + u_t$$

$$= \lambda\alpha + \lambda\beta S_{t-1} + (1-\lambda)I_{t-1} + u_t = \beta_0 + \beta_1 S_{t-1} + \beta_2 I_{t-1} + u_t$$

(c) For consistency we need $E(u_t) = 0$, $E(u_t S_{t-1}) = 0$ and $E(u_t I_{t-1}) = 0$, and the variances of S_t and I_t must be finite (see Property 3.2). These are not, however, enough for BLUE because the model has a lagged dependent variable.

(d) α, β, and λ are estimable. First regress I_t against a constant, S_{t-1}, and I_{t-1} and get $\hat{\beta}_0$, $\hat{\beta}_1$, and $\hat{\beta}_2$. Then $\hat{\lambda} = 1 - \hat{\beta}_2$, $\hat{\alpha} = \hat{\beta}_0/\hat{\lambda}$, and $\hat{\beta} = \hat{\beta}_1/\hat{\lambda}$.

EX 10.5

(a) By an argument similar to that in Exercise 10.3, $\alpha > 0$ and $0 < \beta, \lambda, \mu < 1$.

(b)

$$S_t^* = \alpha + \beta Y_t^*$$

$$S_t = \lambda S_{t-1}^* + (1-\lambda) S_{t-1}$$

$$Y_t^* = \mu Y_{t-1} + (1-\mu) Y_{t-1}^*$$

107

From the first and second equations, $S_t = \lambda(\alpha + \beta\, Y_{t-1}^*) + (1-\lambda)\, S_{t-1}$. This implies that

$$Y_{t-1}^* = \frac{S_t - \lambda\alpha - (1-\lambda)\, S_{t-1}}{\lambda\beta}$$

From this and the third equation

$$\frac{S_{t+1} - \lambda\alpha - (1-\lambda) S_t}{\lambda\beta} = \mu Y_{t-1} + (1-\mu)\frac{S_t - \lambda\alpha - (1-\lambda)\, S_{t-1}}{\lambda\beta}$$

or

$$S_{t+1} - \lambda\alpha - (1-\lambda)\, S_t = \lambda\beta\mu Y_{t-1} + (1-\mu)[S_t - \lambda\alpha - (1-\lambda)\, S_{t-1})]$$

Rearranging terms, using t instead of $t+1$, and adding u_t,

$$\begin{aligned}
S_t &= \lambda\alpha + (1-\lambda)\, S_{t-1} + \lambda\beta\mu Y_{t-2} + (1-\mu)\, S_{t-1} \\
&\quad - \lambda\alpha(1-\mu) - (1-\mu)(1-\lambda)\, S_{t-2} + u_t \\
&= \lambda\alpha\mu + \lambda\beta\mu Y_{t-2} + (2-\lambda-\mu)\, S_{t-1} - (1-\mu)(1-\lambda)\, S_{t-2} + u_t \\
&= \beta_0 + \beta_1 Y_{t-2} + \beta_2 S_{t-1} + \beta_3 S_{t-2} + u_t
\end{aligned}$$

(c) The conditions for consistency are $E(u_t) = E(u_t\, Y_{t-2}) = E(u_t\, S_{t-1}) = E(u_t\, S_{t-2}) = 0$. The estimates are biased because of the presence of two lagged endogenous variables and therefore are not BLUE.

(d) We have $\beta_0 = \lambda\alpha\mu$, $\beta_1 = \lambda\beta\mu$, $\beta_2 = 2-\lambda-\mu$, and $\beta_3 = -(1-\mu)(1-\lambda)$. Let $\lambda_0 = 1-\lambda$ and $\mu_0 = 1-\mu$. The last two equations may be written as $\lambda_0 + \mu_0 = \beta_2$ and $\lambda_0\mu_0 = -\beta_3$. From these, $(\lambda_0-\mu_0)^2 = (\lambda_0+\mu_0)^2 - 4\lambda_0\mu_0 = \beta_2^2 + 4\beta_3$, or $(\lambda_0 - \mu_0) = \pm(\beta_2^2 + 4\beta_3)^{1/2}$. λ and μ are solved from these as

$$\lambda = 1 - \frac{1}{2}\left[\beta_2 \pm (\beta_2^2 + 4\beta_3)^{1/2}\right]$$

$$\mu = 1 - \frac{1}{2}\left[\beta_2 \pm (\beta_2^2 + 4\beta_3)^{1/2}\right]$$

It will be noted that the solutions may not be unique or will not exist unless $\beta_2^2 + 4\beta_3 \geq 0$.

EX 10.6

The following commands and the data file *DATA1010* would be useful in obtaining the necessary output to answer this question.

```
(* EX 10.6, using DATA1010, for Exercise 10.6 *)
genr Yt1 = Yt(-1)
genr Yt2 = Yt(-2)
genr Yt3 = Yt(-3)
genr Yt4 = Yt(-4)
genr Yt5 = Yt(-5)
genr Yt6 = Yt(-6)
corr Yt Yt1 Yt2 Yt3 Yt4 Yt5 Yt6 ;
(* suppress the first 6 observations *)
smpl 1953 ;
ols Ct 0 Yt Yt1 Yt2 Yt3 Yt4 Yt5 Yt6;
(* LM test for AR(1) *)
genr ut = uhat
genr ut1 = ut(-1)
smpl 1954 ;
ols ut 0 ut1 Yt Yt1 Yt2 Yt3 Yt4 Yt5 Yt6;
genr trsq = $nobs*$rsq
pvalue 3 1 trsq
(* reset start date to 1953 and use mixed HILU-CORC *)
smpl 1953 ;
hilu Ct 0 Yt Yt1 Yt2 Yt3 Yt4 Yt5 Yt6;
genr temp = coeff(Yt) + coeff(Yt1) + coeff(Yt2) + coeff(Yt3)
genr mult = temp + coeff(Yt4) + coeff(Yt5) + coeff(Yt6)
print mult;
```

As may be expected, there is a great deal of multicollinearity among the explanatory variables with pairwise correlations 0.989 or higher. As a result, most of the coefficients are insignificant with the exception of that for *Yt*. This result holds even though the LM test for first-order autocorrelation indicated significance and the model was reestimated with the mixed HILU-

CORC method. The long-run multiplier is the sum of the coefficients for Y terms and is 0.943.

EX 10.7

The relevant model for this is given in equation (10.10). The commands for obtaining the empirical results are as follows.

```
(* EX 10.7, using DATA1010, for Exercise 10.7 *)
genr Ct1 = Ct(-1)
genr Yt1 = Yt(-1)
corr Ct1 Yt1 ;
(* suppress the first observation *)
smpl 1948 ;
ols Ct 0 Ct1 Yt1 ;
(* LM test for AR(1) *)
genr ut = uhat
genr ut1 = ut(-1)
smpl 1949 ;
ols ut 0 ut1 Ct1 Yt1 ;
genr trsq = $nobs*$rsq
pvalue 3 1 trsq
(* reset start date to 1948 and use mixed HILU-CORC *)
smpl 1948 ;
hilu Ct 0 Ct1 Yt1 ;
```

The LM test for first-order serial correlation indicates its presence and hence the mixed HILU-CORC procedure is appropriate. The estimates and associated statistics are presented in the next page.

The estimates of the original model are given by $\hat{\lambda} = 1 - \hat{\beta}_1 = 1 - 0.974 = 0.026$. $\hat{\alpha} = \hat{\beta}_0 / \hat{\lambda} = 14340/0.026 = 551577$. $\hat{\beta} = \hat{\beta}_2 / \hat{\lambda} = -0.571/0.026 = -21.962$. The estimates are nonsensical and unacceptable, especially the large negative value for the marginal propensity to consume out of expected income. Two possible reasons are (1) high multicollinearity between $Ct1$ and $Yt1$ and (2) the fact that $\hat{\rho} = 0.99$ and is too close to 1 suggesting the possibility of a unit root. As we saw in the text, unit roots tend to make variances large and hence estimates might be unreliable.

VARIABLE	COEFFICIENT	STDERROR	T STAT	PROB t > |T|
constant	14340.51643	3410.51103	4.205	0.0001 ***
Ct1	0.97434	0.22738	4.285	0.0001 ***
Yt1	-0.57127	0.19976	-2.860	0.0068 ***

Adjusted R-squared computed as the square of the corr. between observed and predicted dep. var. is 0.997.

EX 10.8

For the empirical analysis of this question use the same data file and the following ECSLIB commands.

```
(* EX 10.8, using DATA1010, for Exercise 10.8 *)
genr time
genr lnCt1 = ln(Ct(-1))
(* generate first difference in the log as in equation (10.13) *)
genr DCt = ldiff(Ct)
genr DCt1 = DCt(-1)
genr DCt2 = DCt(-2)
genr DCt3 = DCt(-3)
genr DCt4 = DCt(-4)
genr DCt5 = DCt(-5)
genr DCt6 = DCt(-6)
(* estimate the Dickey-Fuller test regression *)
smpl 1954 ;
ols DCt 0 time lnCt1 DCt1 DCt2 DCt3 DCt4 DCt5 DCt6 ;
omit time lnCt1 ;
(* Redo analysis with Yt instead of Ct *)
smpl 1947 ;
```

111

```
genr lnYt1 = ln(Yt(-1))
genr DYt = ldiff(Yt)
genr DYt1 = DYt(-1)
genr DYt2 = DYt(-2)
genr DYt3 = DYt(-3)
genr DYt4 = DYt(-4)
genr DYt5 = DYt(-5)
genr DYt6 = DYt(-6)
(* estimate the Dickey-Fuller test regression *)
smpl 1954 ;
ols DYt 0 time lnYt1 DYt1 DYt2 DYt3 DYt4 DYt5 DYt6 ;
omit time lnYt1 ;
```

The unrestricted model for the unit root test is given by equation (10.13). F-statistics for the Dickey-Fuller test are given as 2.017 for consumption and as 1.889 for income. From Table 10.4 we note that the test statistics are below the critical values for levels at or below 10 percent. Thus unit root cannot be rejected in either case. A modified model could be the error correction model described in Section 10.3 and carried out in the next exercise.

EX 10.9

The relevant ECSLIB commands for the error correction model are given below.

```
(* EX 10.9, using DATA1010, for Exercise 10.9 *)
genr LDCt = ldiff(Ct)
genr LDYt = ldiff(Yt)
genr LY_C = ln(Yt(-1)) - ln(Ct(-1))
smpl 1948 ;
ols LDCt 0 LDYt LY_C ;
```

The short-run adjustment coefficient is 0.253 with a t-statistic of 2.889 which is highly significant.

EX 10.10

This exercise is carried out only with the data set in Table 10.12 (which is in the file *DATA1012*). The relevant commands are as follows.

```
(* EX 10.10, using DATA1012, for Exercise 10.10 *)
genr time
(* generate first difference in the log as in equation (10.13) *)
genr lnpop1 = ln(pop(-1))
genr Dpop = ldiff(pop)
genr Dpop1 = Dpop(-1)
genr Dpop2 = Dpop(-2)
genr Dpop3 = Dpop(-3)
genr Dpop4 = Dpop(-4)
genr Dpop5 = Dpop(-5)
genr Dpop6 = Dpop(-6)
(* estimate the Dickey-Fuller test regression *)
smpl 1967 ;
ols Dpop 0 time lnpop1 Dpop1 Dpop2 Dpop3 Dpop4 Dpop5 Dpop6 ;
omit time lnpop1 ;
```

The *F*-statistic for the Dickey-Fuller test for unit root is given by 3.498 which is not significant even at the 10 percent level. The presence of a unit root is therefore suggested.

EX 10.11
The following *ECŜLIB* commands will be useful in carrying out the empirical analysis for this.

```
(* EX 10.11, using DATA9.1, for Exercise 10.11 *)
genr time
genr Yt = farmpop
genr Yt1 =Yt(-1)
genr Yt2 =Yt(-2)
smpl 1949 ;
```

```
ols Yt 0 Yt1 Yt2 time ;
genr ua = uhat
ols Yt 0 Yt1 Yt2 ;
smpl 1948 ;
ols Yt 0 Yt1 time;
genr ub = uhat
ols Yt 0 Yt1 ;
lags ua ub;
smpl 1950 ;
ols ua 0 Yt1 Yt2 time ua_1 ;
genr trsq1 = $nobs*$rsq
pvalue 3 1 trsq1
smpl 1949 ;
ols ub 0 Yt1 time ub_1 ;
genr trsq2 = $nobs*$rsq
pvalue 3 1 trsq2
```

In terms of the model selection statistics, the first model (call it Model A) with two lags is better than the second one (Model B) and a third one in which the *time* variable is omitted). The Durbin-*h* test is applicable only for Model B. The test statistic is (see Section 10.2)

$$ h = \hat{\rho} \left[\frac{T'}{1 - T's_{\beta}^2} \right]^{\frac{1}{2}} $$

where $\hat{\rho}$ is the first order autocorrelation, $T' = 36$, and $s_{\hat{\beta}}$ is the standard error for the coefficient of Y_{t-1}. For Model B, $T' = 36$, $\hat{\rho} = -0.282$, $s_{\hat{\beta}} = 0.03055$, and hence $h = -1.72$. From Table A.1 we see that the area to the right of this in the standard normal distribution is 0.0427 (0.5 - 0.4573) < 0.05 and hence there is significant serial correlation in the second model.

The LM test statistics for the two models are, respectively, 8.088 and 3.997. From the *p*-values it is easy to verify that these statistics are significant at the 5 percent level thus supporting the Durbin-*h* test. Because serial correlation is present and there are lagged endogenous variables, OLS estimates are not consistent.

EX 10.12

(a)   From Chapter 5, multicollinearity makes standard errors larger, but esti-
        mates are still unbiased, consistent, and most efficient (BLUE). Ignor-
        ing serial correlation, however, makes estimates inefficient. Similarly,
        adding an irrelevant variables also makes estimates inefficient. The
        results are thus not similar (that is, the statement is false).

(b)   Model B has Y_{t-1} which is generally highly correlated with Y_t. We
        would therefore expect it to have a higher R^2 than Model A (that is, the
        statement is true).

(c)   We saw in Section 10.2 that the presence of a lagged dependent variable
        generally results in a higher DW statistic (d) than one without the
        lagged variable. If even this higher d is less than d_L, serial correlation is
        indicated. The statement is therefore true.

EX 10.13

(a)   To get the empirical results using ECSLIB, create a batch file, call it
        ex10-13.inp, containing the lines listed below. Then use the DOS com-
        mand

        ecslib -v50 data9-13 < ex10-13.inp > ex10-13.out

        (* EX 10.13, using DATA9-13, for Exercise 10.13 *)
        lags Mt Gt Tt Xt;
        smpl 1960.1;
        ols Yt 0 Mt Gt Tt Xt Mt_1 Mt_2 Mt_3 Mt_4 Gt_1 Gt_2 Gt_3
         Gt_4 Tt_1 Tt_2 Tt_3 Tt_4 Xt_1 Xt_2 Xt_3 Xt_4 ;
        hilu Yt 0 Mt Gt Tt Xt Mt_1 Mt_2 Mt_3 Mt_4 Gt_1 Gt_2 Gt_3
         Gt_4 Tt_1 Tt_2 Tt_3 Tt_4 Xt_1 Xt_2 Xt_3 Xt_4 ;
        genr M1 = Mt + Mt_1 + Mt_2 + Mt_3 + Mt_4
        genr M2 = Mt_1 + (2*Mt_2) + (3*Mt_3) + (4*Mt_4)

```
genr M3 = Mt_1 + (4*Mt_2) + (9*Mt_3) + (16*Mt_4)
genr M4 = Mt_1 + (8*Mt_2) + (27*Mt_3) + (64*Mt_4)
genr G1 = Gt + Gt_1 + Gt_2 + Gt_3 + Gt_4
genr G2 = Gt_1 + (2*Gt_2) + (3*Gt_3) + (4*Gt_4)
genr G3 = Gt_1 + (4*Gt_2) + (9*Gt_3) + (16*Gt_4)
genr G4 = Gt_1 + (8*Gt_2) + (27*Gt_3) + (64*Gt_4)
genr T1 = Tt + Tt_1 + Tt_2 + Tt_3 + Tt_4
genr T2 = Tt_1 + (2*Tt_2) + (3*Tt_3) + (4*Tt_4)
genr T3 = Tt_1 + (4*Tt_2) + (9*Tt_3) + (16*Tt_4)
genr T4 = Tt_1 + (8*Tt_2) + (27*Tt_3) + (64*Tt_4)
genr X1 = Xt + Xt_1 + Xt_2 + Xt_3 + Xt_4
genr X2 = Xt_1 + (2*Xt_2) + (3*Xt_3) + (4*Xt_4)
genr X3 = Xt_1 + (4*Xt_2) + (9*Xt_3) + (16*Xt_4)
genr X4 = Xt_1 + (8*Xt_2) + (27*Xt_3) + (64*Xt_4)
ols Yt 0 M1 M2 M3 G1 G2 G3 T1 T2 T3 X1 X2 X3 ;
ols Yt 0 M1 M2 M3 M4 G1 G2 G3 G4 T1 T2 T3 T4 X1
 X2 X3 X4 ;
smpl 1959.1;
ols Yt 0 Mt Gt Tt Xt;
genr ut = uhat
genr Yt_1 = Yt(-1)
smpl 1959.2;
ols ut 0 Mt Gt Tt Xt Yt_1;
genr trsq = $nobs*$rsq
pvalue 3 1 trsq ;
ols Yt 0 Mt Gt Tt Xt Yt_1;
```

The model selection statistics are much worse compared to the model in Exercise 9.10 which had no lags. Also, almost all the lagged variables (the only exception being M_{t-1}) are statistically insignificant. The main reason for this is the strong multicollinearity among all the variables. The Durbin-Watson statistic is 0.471 and indicates the presence of serial correlation. CORC estimates do not improve the results much because multicollinearity is still a problem here. The sign of the regression coefficient for taxes is positive which is counterintuitive.

(b)   In five out of the eight model selection criteria the Almon lag model with a cubic does better than a quadratic specification. However, the static model with no lags outperforms them all. Presumably multicollinearity is still a problem.

(c)   For simplicity, the basic model is the static model used in Exercise 9.10, with no lags. $(T-1)R^2$ for the auxiliary regression is 51.011 which is very highly significant. This means that Y_{t-1} belongs in the model. The model with Y_{t-1} in it is considerably better, in terms of the model selection criteria, than all the other models. This is not surprising because Y_t and Y_{t-1} are very highly correlated.

(d)   The long-run multiplier is the sum of the regression coefficients when there is no lagged dependent variable. For the model in part (a) the monetary multiplier is 0.91217 - 0.98873 + 0.23351 + 0.18489 - 0.18683 = 0.155. Similarly, the multipliers for G, T, and X are, respectively, 0.465, 1.92, and 1.988. For the model with Y_{t-1} in it, the long-run multiplier is given in equation (9.11). We have, for M, G, T, and X, 0.282, -1.368, 3.099, and 1.863. The multipliers for G and T have unexpected signs and the values are not credible. The calculations for the Almon lag models are tedious but the procedure is the same. The multipliers for G and T are not believable in most of the models.

(e)   Although the model selection criteria would choose the model in (c) with the Y_{t-1} term as the "best", none of the models is acceptable. The signs and magnitudes of the regression coefficients for G and T are not credible, suggesting that the models are misspecified.

EX 10.14
Data file *DATA9-12* and the following ECSLIB commands will be useful in obtaining the necessary empirical results.

```
(* EX 10.14, using DATA9-12, for Exercise 10.14 *)
logs QNC PRICE INCOME PRIME UNEMP;
genr l_QNC_1=l_QNC(-1)
smpl 1970.2 ;
```

ols l_QNC 0 l_QNC_1 l_PRICE l_INCOME l_PRIME l_UNEMP
STRIKE SPRING;

From Section 10.1 the partial adjustment mechanism yields the lagged dependent variable Y_{t-1}. Inclusion of $\ln(QNC_{t-1})$ in the model does not improve the model. Most of the model selection statistics are worse and the lagged dependent variable is statistically insignificant. The long-run elasticities for PRICE, INCOME, PRIME and UNEMP are -0.375, 1.177, -0.346, and -0.453, all of which are reasonable.

EX 10.15
The relevant ECSLIB commands are as follows.

```
(* EX 10.15, using DATA9-12, for Exercise 10.15 *)
logs STOCK PRICE INCOME PRIME UNEMP;
genr l_STOCK1=l_STOCK(-1)
ols l_STOCK 0 l_PRICE l_INCOME l_PRIME l_UNEMP STRIKE
 SPRING;
smpl 1970.2 ;
ols l_STOCK 0 l_STOCK1 l_PRICE l_INCOME l_PRIME l_UNEMP
STRIKE SPRING;
```

The partial adjustment model does much better, in terms of model selection criteria, than a model without the lagged dependent variable. However, most of the variables which were significant in the second model become insignificant when the lagged dependent variable is included.

EX 10.16

(a) Taking logarithms we get $\ln P_t = \ln K + \ln M_t - \ln N_t$ or $p_t = k + m_t - n_t$. This gives $\Delta p_t = \Delta m_t - \Delta n_t$.

(b) $p_t = \beta_0 + \beta_1 p_{t-1} + \beta_2 m_t + \beta_3 m_{t-1} + \beta_4 n_t + \beta_5 n_{t-1} + u_t$. Substitute $\beta_1 = 1-\gamma$, $\beta_3 = \gamma-\beta_2$, and $\beta_5 = -\gamma-\beta_4$. We have,

$$p_t = \beta_0 + (1-\gamma)p_{t-1} + \beta_2\, m_t + (\gamma-\beta_2)m_{t-1} + \beta_4\, n_t - (\gamma+\beta_4)\, n_{t-1} + u_t$$

which gives

$$\Delta p_t = \beta_0 + \beta_2\, \Delta m_t + \beta_4\, \Delta n_t - \gamma(p_{t-1} - m_{t-1} + n_{t-1}) + u_t$$

In the long run, the change in variables is zero. This reduces to $p^* = k_0 + m^* - n^*$, which is of the form in part (a).

(c)   The model derived in part (b) is the error-correction model. If $\gamma \neq 0$ there is support for the error-correction mechanism. The empirical results may be obtained with the following *ECSLIB* commands and the data file *DATA1011*.

```
(* EX 10.16, using DATA1011, for Exercise 10.16 *)
lags N M P;
genr DN = diff(N)
genr DM = diff(M)
genr DP = diff(P)
genr Z = P_1 - M_1 + N_1
smpl 1960 ;
ols DP 0 DM DN Z;
omit Z;
omit DN;
```

We note that $\hat{\gamma}$ is not significantly different from zero. Thus there is no support for the error-correction mechanism. It is interesting that if the last variable is omitted only the money supply term is statistically significant. Change in population does not appear to matter in explaining changes in the price level.

CHAPTER 11

PRACTICE PROBLEMS

PP 11.1

While forecasting, u_t is set to zero because it is unpredictable. All the log models have the term $\hat{\sigma}^2/2$ to correct for the bias discussed in Section 11.4. The desired formulas are obtained by simply exponentiating the log models.

Log-linear: Whether $\hat{\beta}_o$ is positive, zero, or negative, the shape of the relation between $\hat{Y}_t$ and t is the same. If $\hat{\beta}_1 > 0$ the relationship is an exponentially increasing function starting at $e^{\hat{\beta}_o + (\hat{\sigma}^2/2)}$. If $\hat{\beta}_1 < 0$ the graph will be exponentially decreasing to zero. If $\hat{\beta}_1 = 0$, we get a horizontal line.

Double-log: Here also the sign of $\hat{\beta}_1$ determines the shape. If $\hat{\beta}_1 = 0$ we have a horizontal line. The slope of the function is

$$\frac{d\hat{Y}_t}{dt} = e^{\hat{\beta}_o + (\hat{\sigma}^2/2)} \hat{\beta}_1 t^{\hat{\beta}_1 - 1}$$

If $\hat{\beta}_1 > 1$ this slope is always positive. Hence $\hat{Y}_t$ steadily increases at an increasing rate. If $0 < \hat{\beta}_1 < 1$ then also $\hat{Y}_t$ increases, but at a decreasing rate. If $\hat{\beta}_1 < 0$, then $d\hat{Y}_t/dt$ is negative and hence $\hat{Y}_t$ steadily decreases to zero.

Logistic: If $\hat{\beta}_1 > 0$ the graph will be as in Figure 4.1. When $\hat{\beta}_1$ is negative, the shape will be a mirror image, decreasing steadily and with a point of inflection.

PP 11.2

First create a batch file called *pp11-2.inp* containing the following lines.

```
(* PP 11.2, using DATA11-1, for Practice Problem 11.2 *)
genr time
genr tsq = time*time
genr t3 = tsq*time
genr invt = 1/time
```

```
genr logit = wages/(20-wages)
logs wages time logit ;
graph wages time ;
(* linear Model A *)
smpl 1960 1985
ols wages 0 time ;
(* Note that the OLS estimates exhibit serial correlation *)
hilu wages 0 time;
fcast 1986 1989 yhata
smpl 1986 1989
print -o wages yhata ;
ols wages 0 yhata;
(* quadratic Model B *)
smpl 1960 1985
hilu wages 0 time tsq;
fcast 1986 1989 yhatb
smpl 1986 1989
print -o wages yhatb ;
ols wages 0 yhatb;
(* cubic Model C *)
smpl 1960 1985
hilu wages 0 time tsq t3;
fcast 1986 1989 yhatc
smpl 1986 1989
print -o wages yhatc ;
ols wages 0 yhatc ;
(* linear-log Model D *)
smpl 1960 1985
hilu wages 0 l_time;
fcast 1986 1989 yhatd
smpl 1986 1989
print -o wages yhatd ;
ols wages 0 yhatd ;
(* reciprocal Model E *)
smpl 1960 1985
```

```
hilu wages 0 invt;
fcast 1986 1989 yhate
smpl 1986 1989
print -o wages yhate ;
ols wages 0 yhate ;
(*  log-linear Model F  *)
smpl 1960 1985
hilu l_wages 0 time;
fcast 1986 1989 yhatf ;
smpl 1986 1989
genr T = 4
genr yhatf = exp(yhatf+(0.000371/2))
print -o wages yhatf ;
genr uhatf = wages - yhatf
genr essf = T*mean(uhatf*uhatf)
criteria essf T 2
ols wages 0 yhatf ;
(*  double-log Model G  *)
smpl 1960 1985
hilu l_wages 0 l_time ;
fcast 1986 1989 yhatg
smpl 1986 1989
genr yhatg = exp(yhatg+(0.000525/2))
print -o wages yhatg ;
genr uhatg = wages - yhatg
genr essg = T*mean(uhatg*uhatg)
criteria essg T 2
ols wages 0 yhatg ;
(*  logistic Model H  *)
smpl 1960 1985
hilu l_logit 0 time;
fcast 1986 1989 temp
smpl 1986 1989
genr temp = exp(temp+(0.000853/2))
genr yhath = 20*temp/(1+temp)
```

```
genr uhath = wages - yhath
genr essh =  T*mean(uhath*uhath)
criteria essh T 2 ;
print -o wages yhatg ;
ols wages 0 yhath ;
```

Next execute the DOS command

$$\text{ecslib -v50 data11-1} \; < \; \text{pp11-2.inp} \; > \text{pp11-2.out}$$

For each of the forecasts, an equation of the form $Y_t = a + b \, Y_t^f$ was estimated as described in Section 11.2. If the forecast was perfect, we would expect a to be zero and b to 1. The following table summarizes the values of a and b and the corresponding $\overline{R}^2$ for the above regression.

Model	$\hat{a}$	$\hat{b}$	$\overline{R}^2$
A	1.50725	0.83304	0.709
B	2.81841	0.70657	0.782
C	- 4.31752	1.43170	0.185
D	1.00351	0.90177	0.684
E	1.01956	0.90393	0.683
F	2.81774	0.69854	0.760
G	1.29460	0.85409	0.684
H	1.60813	0.82521	0.737

Although the goodness of fit is reasonable for out of sample performance, they all suffer from bias due to the fact that none of the values for a is near zero. The quadratic model B has the best overall fit but it suffers from serious bias. In that dimension Models D and E are good.

PP 11.3

(a) The first difference is
$$\Delta Y_t = Y_t - Y_{t-1} = \alpha + \beta t + \gamma t^2 - \alpha - \beta(t-1) - \gamma(t-1)^2 = \beta + \gamma(2t-1)$$
The second difference is therefore
$$\Delta^2 Y_t = \beta - \gamma + 2\gamma t - \left[(\beta - \gamma) + 2\gamma(t-1)\right] = 2\gamma$$
which is constant and is hence stationary.

(b) Let $Y_t = \alpha + \beta t$. Then
$$\Delta_i = Y_t - Y_{t-i} = \alpha + \beta t - \left[\alpha + \beta(t - i)\right] = \beta i$$
which is constant. Hence Δ_i is stationary.

EXERCISES

EX 11.1
Sections 11.1 and 11.3 have the appropriate definitions.

EX 11.2
See Section 11.2.

EX 11.3
The first step is to regress (using sample period data) actual Y_t against a constant, f_{t1}, f_{t2}, and f_{t3} and obtain the weights $\hat{\beta}_o, \hat{\beta}_1, \hat{\beta}_2$, and $\hat{\beta}_3$. Next obtain h-step ahead forecasts $f_{t+h,1}$, $f_{t+h,2}$, and $f_{t+h,3}$. The combined h-step ahead forecast is $f_{t+h} = \hat{\beta}_0 + \hat{\beta}_1 f_{t+h,1} + \hat{\beta}_2 f_{t+h,2} + \hat{\beta}_3 f_{t+h,3}$.

EX 11.4
Deseasonalizing refers to the process of removing the seasonal effects from a series. Define seasonal dummy variables D_1, D_2, and D_3 which take the value 1 during the first, second, and third quarters respectively, and 0 in other quarters. Next regress sales (S_t) against a constant, D_1, D_2, and D_3. The deseasonalized series is given by $S_t^* = S_t - \hat{\beta}_o - \hat{\beta}_1 D_1 - \hat{\beta}_2 D_2 - \hat{\beta}_3 D_3$, where the $\hat{\beta}$'s are the estimated regression coefficients.

124

EX 11.5

Detrending stands for the process of removing a time trend from a series. First graph Y_t against time and identify the shape of the relationship (see Section 11.4 for possible functional form). Let $f(t)$ be the fitted function. Then the detrended series is $Y_t^* = Y_t - f(t)$. For example if a quadratic relation was fit, the detrended series will be $Y_t^* = Y_t - \hat{\beta}_o - \hat{\beta}_1 t - \hat{\beta}_2 t^2$, where the $\hat{\beta}$'s are the estimated regression coefficients.

EX 11.7

$Var(u_t) = Var(\varepsilon_t - \lambda\varepsilon_{t-1}) = \sigma^2(1 + \lambda^2)$. $Cov(u_t, u_{t-1}) = Cov(\varepsilon_t - \lambda\varepsilon_{t-1}, \varepsilon_{t-1} - \lambda\varepsilon_{t-2}) = -\lambda\sigma^2$. Finally, $Cov(u_t, u_{t-s}) = 0$ for all $s > 1$ because ε_t is a white noise series. Therefore the only non-zero correlation is with $t-1$ for which the correlation coefficient is $-\lambda/(1 + \lambda^2)$. It is easy to extend this analysis to prove that if the moving average is of order p, the first p autocorrelation values will be non-zero but the rest will be zero.

EX 11.9

See Section 11.7 for the definition of *stationarity*.

Taking logarithms of both sides of the relation, $\ln(Y_t) = \ln(Y_o) + \lambda t$. First difference in logs is

$$\Delta\ln(Y_t) = \ln(Y_t) - \ln(Y_{t-1}) = \lambda$$

which is constant and hence is stationary.

EX 11.11

The first step is to decide on the differencing. Use the Ljung-Box test in equation (11.25) to check whether the series is stationary. If it is not, graph it against time. If the series exhibits a linear trend, difference once. If the trend is quadratic, difference twice. If the trend is exponential, take logarithms first and then difference. Test for stationarity at each stage. If seasonality is present, deseasonalize the series.

Next graph the correlogram. If it remains near zero after a certain lag, then that is the approximate choice for the moving average order. Then graph the

125

partial correlogram. If it remains near zero after a certain lag, then that is the order of autoregression. If neither of these happens but both plots eventually decline to zero, start with an ARMA(1, 1) model.

The model is next estimated using a maximum likelihood estimation program. After estimating the model test whether the residual errors are white noise. The orders of autoregression and moving average can also be changed and the new model tested to see if it predicts better.

EX 11.12
The procedure is very much like the one adopted in Practice Problem 11.2.

EX 11.13
Use Exercise 10.8 as an example for this question.

EX 11.14
To obtain the results for this question use the data file *DATA9-13* and the following ECSLIB commands.

```
(* EX  11.14, using DATA9-13, for Exercise 11.14 *)
genr time
lags Yt Mt;
genr dYt = diff(Yt)
genr dMt = diff(Mt)
lags dYt dMt ;
smpl 1959.3 ;
ols dYt 0 time Yt_1 dYt_1 ;
omit time Yt_1 ;
ols dMt 0 time Mt_1 dMt_1 ;
omit time Mt_1 ;
smpl 1959.1 ;
ols Yt 0 Mt;
genr ut = uhat
genr ut1 = ut(-1)
genr diffut = diff(ut)
```

```
genr diffut_1 = diffut(-1)
genr diffut_2 = diffut(-2)
genr diffut_3 = diffut(-3)
genr diffut_4 = diffut(-4)
smpl 1960.2 ;
ols diffut ut1 diffut_1 diffut_2 diffut_3 diffut_4 ;
```

F-statistics for the Dickey-Fuller test for unit roots are 14.162 and 14.039 for GNP and money supply. We see from Table 10.4 that these values are significant at the 1 percent level. Thus we reject the null hypothesis of unit root.

From the cointegration regression, the DW statistic is 0.097 which is not significant even at the 10 percent (see Table 11.8). The t-statistic for $\hat{u}_{t-1}$ in the Dickey-Fuller regression is 0.766 in absolute value. This too is insignificant Thus, there is some no evidence of cointegration.

EX 11.15
The data file *DATA10-9* and the following commands will be useful o obtain the empirical results for this question.

```
(*  EX 11.15, using DATA10-9, for Exercise 11.15   *)
genr ml=um*100/gnpdef
genr g=ug*100/gnpdef
genr time
lags ml g;
genr dml = diff(ml)
genr dg = diff(g)
lags dml dg ;
smpl 1942 ;
ols dml 0 time ml_1 dml_1 ;
omit time ml_1 ;
ols dg 0 time g_1 dg_1 ;
omit time g_1 ;
smpl 1940 ;
```

```
ols ml 0 g;
genr ut = uhat
genr ut1 = ut(-1)
genr diffut = diff(ut)
genr diffut_1 = diffut(-1)
genr diffut_2 = diffut(-2)
genr diffut_3 = diffut(-3)
genr diffut_4 = diffut(-4)
smpl 1945 ;
ols diffut ut1 diffut_1 diffut_2 diffut_3 diffut_4 ;
```

F-statistics for the Dickey-Fuller test for unit roots are 22.913 and 10.820 for military and total government expenditures. We see from Table 10.4 that these values are significant at the 1 percent level. Thus we reject the null hypothesis of unit root.

From the cointegration regression, the DW statistic is 0.377 which is significant at the 10 percent level but not at the 5 percent level (see Table 11.8). The t-statistic for $\hat{u}_{t-1}$ in the Dickey-Fuller regression is 2.867 in absolute value. This too is significant at the 10 percent level but not at the 5 percent level. Thus, there is some evidence of cointegration, but it is not very strong.

CHAPTER 12

EXERCISES

EX 12.3

The dependent variable is not binary here but is a fraction. Therefore the logit model would be more appropriate. First compute $Z = \ln[H/(1-H)]$ and regress Z against a constant, Y, P, and R.

EX 12.4

Since we want to know whether a particular employee joins the union or not, we would want to survey individual employees. However, we would also choose several companies and survey their employees. As in the application in Section 12.2 the logit model in equation (12.3) would be appropriate with a general maximum likelihood procedure. Several characteristics of the individual will be measured; age, gender, race, education, skill level or occupational status, income, and so on. Across companies some variables will differ; union membership fee, percentage of workers who are already union members, etc.

EX 12.5

The linear probability model or the logit model would be appropriate, but the logit model is preferable because of the problems that a linear probability model creates. Let P be the probability of conviction. For individual observations P will be 1 or 0. Equation (12.2) would be estimated because in equation (12.1) $P/(1-P)$ is undefined.

The number of previous arrests will clearly increase the probability of conviction. It is often argued that a well-educated white person with a high income is likely to be acquitted or released on probation. If this perception is valid, the probability of conviction will decrease when education and income increase or when a person is white. In principle, the gender should be irrelevant to the probability of conviction.

EX 12.6

This is an example of the Tobit model. The model is

$$W = \beta_o + \beta_1 \, AGE + \beta_2 \, EDUC + \beta_3 \, EXP + \beta_4 RACE$$

$$+ \beta_5 \, CLER + \beta_6 \, PROF + u$$

for those who are employed, and $W = 0$ for others. AGE is the age, EDUC is education, EXP is experience, $RACE = 1$ for white, $CLER = 1$ for a clerical worker, and $PROF = 1$ for a professional work. The unskilled group is the control. The maximum likelihood procedure will be applied here to a likelihood function similar to the one in Section 12.4.

CHAPTER 13

PRACTICE PROBLEMS

PP 13.1
Substituting equations (13.4) through (13.6) in (13.7) we get,

$$Y_t = \alpha_0 + \alpha_1(Y_t - T_t) + \alpha_2(Y_{t-1} - T_{t-1}) + u_t + \beta_0$$
$$+ \beta_1(Y_t - T_t) + \beta_2(Y_{t-1} - T_{t-1}) + v_t$$

Rregrouping terms, this becomes

$$(1 - \alpha_1 - \beta_1)Y_t = \alpha_0 + (\alpha_2 + \beta_2)Y_{t-1} - (\alpha_1 + \beta_1)T_t - (\alpha_2 + \beta_2)T_{t-1}$$
$$+ G_t + u_t + v_t$$

The reduced form equation for Y_t is therefore given by

$$Y_t = \frac{\alpha_0}{1 - \alpha_1 - \beta_1} + \frac{\alpha_2 + \beta_2}{1 - \alpha_1 - \beta_1} Y_{t-1} - \frac{\alpha_1 + \beta_1}{1 - \alpha_1 - \beta_1} T_t$$

$$- \frac{\alpha_2 + \beta_2}{1 - \alpha_1 - \beta_1} T_{t-1} + \frac{G_t + u_t + v_t}{1 - \alpha_1 - \beta_1}$$

$$= \pi_0 + \pi_1 Y_{t-1} + \pi_2 T_t + \pi_3 T_{t-1} + \pi_4 G_t + error$$

The other reduced form equations are easily derived from this.

PP 13.2
It will be noted that the second and third equations are self-contained and do not have Y_1. They can be solved jointly for Y_2 and Y_3. Substituting for Y_2 from the second equation into the third equation, we can solve for Y_3 as

$$Y_3 = \frac{\gamma_0 + \gamma_1 \beta_0}{1 - \gamma_1 \beta_1} + \frac{\gamma_1 \beta_2}{1 - \gamma_1 \beta_1} X_1 + error = \theta_0 + \theta_1 X_1 + error$$

Using this in the second equation and grouping terms, we get

$$Y_2 = (\beta_0 + \beta_1\theta_0) + (\beta_1\theta_1 + \beta_2)X_1 + error$$

$$= \mu_0 + \mu_1 X_1 + error$$

Next, substitute for Y_2 and Y_3 in the first equation.

$$Y_1 = \alpha_0 + \alpha_1(\mu_0 + \mu_1 X_1) + \alpha_2(\theta_0 + \theta_1 X_1) + \alpha_4 X_1 + \alpha_5 X_2 + error$$

Solving for the reduced form for Y_1, we get

$$Y_1 = (\alpha_0 + \alpha_1\mu_0 + \alpha_2\theta_0) + (\alpha_1\mu_1 + \alpha_2\theta_1 + \alpha_4)X_1 + \alpha_5 X_2 + error$$

$$= \lambda_0 + \lambda_1 X_1 + \lambda_2 X_2 + error$$

EXERCISES

EX 13.2

From Section 13.5 the ILS estimate of β is given by $\tilde{\beta} = S_{CI}/(S_{CI} + S_{II})$. Applying OLS to the reduced form equation for Y_t, we get $\hat{\mu}_1 = S_{YI}/S_{II}$ by proceeding as we did in Chapter 3. From equation (13.14) we see that $\hat{\mu}_1 = 1/(1-\hat{\beta})$. Hence the ILS estimate is

$$\hat{\beta} = \frac{\hat{\mu}_1 - 1}{\hat{\mu}_1} = \frac{S_{YI} - S_{II}}{S_{YI}}$$

Because $Y = C + I$, we have

$$S_{YI} = \Sigma(Y - \bar{Y})(I - \bar{I}) = \Sigma\left[(C - \bar{C}) + (I - \bar{I})\right](I - \bar{I}) = S_{CI} + S_{II}$$

Hence $\hat{\beta} = (S_{YI} - S_{II})/S_{YI} = S_{CI}/(S_{CI} + S_{II})$, which is the same as $\tilde{\beta}$. Therefore ILS can be applied to the reduced form of either C_t or Y_t.

EX 13.4

(a) Because these are three endogenous variables, at least two variables must be absent in each equation. In the second equation A and X are absent. In the third equation M, Y, and U are excluded. The third equation is therefore over-identified. The second equation is exactly identified.

(b) The equation for M is already in the reduced form. We have

$$A = X - M = (\beta_1 - \alpha_1) - \alpha_2 Y + (\beta_2 - \alpha_3)P + \beta_3 A - \alpha_4 U + v - u$$

Solving for A we get the reduce form for A as

$$A = \frac{\beta_1 - \alpha_1}{1 - \beta_3} - \frac{\alpha_2 Y}{1 - \beta_3} + \frac{\beta_2 - \alpha_3}{1 - \beta_3}P - \frac{\alpha_4 U}{1 - \beta_3} + \frac{v - u}{1 - \beta_3}$$

The reduced form for X is

$$X = \beta_1 + \beta_2 P + \beta_3 \left[\frac{\beta_1 - \alpha_1}{1 - \beta_3} - \frac{\alpha_2 Y}{1 - \beta_3} + \frac{\beta_2 - \alpha_3}{1 - \beta_3}P \right.$$

$$\left. - \frac{\alpha_4 U}{1 - \beta_3} + \frac{v - u}{1 - \beta_3} \right] + v$$

$$= \frac{\beta_1 - \beta_3 \alpha_1}{1 - \beta_3} + \frac{\beta_2 - \beta_3 \alpha_3}{1 - \beta_3}P - \frac{\beta_3 \alpha_2}{1 - \beta_3}Y$$

$$- \frac{\beta_3 \alpha_4 U}{1 - \beta_3} + \frac{v - \beta_3 u}{1 - \beta_3}$$

(c) First regress A against a constant, Y, P, and U, and save $\hat{A}$. Next regress X against a constant P, and $\hat{A}$ to obtain $\hat{\beta}_1, \hat{\beta}_2$, and $\hat{\beta}_3$.

(d) The second equation has no other endogenous variables and is hence already in the reduced form. Therefore OLS will give estimates which are unbiased, consistent, and efficient.

(e) Because A is correlated with v, OLS estimates of the third equation will be biased and inconsistent.

EX 13.5

(a) If homes are expensive, they are targets for burglaries and hence pro- perty crime can be expected to increase (that is, $\alpha_2 > 0$). If POPDEN is high, there are two effects. There may be more houses to burgle and hence POPCRIME might go up. But if an area is dense, more people might be alert and report crimes. The sign of α_3 is therefore ambiguous. If unemployment rate is high more people might turn to crime ($\alpha_4 > 0$). If more police are around, crime is likely to be less ($\alpha_5 < 0$, and $\beta_2 < 0$).

133

Death penalty is likely to reduce violent crimes ($\beta_3 < 0$). The effect of age is ambiguous. If crime is up, a municipality is likely to hire more police officers. Hence we would expect γ_2 and γ_3 to be positive.

(b) We need two variables to be absent from each equation. The first equation has DEATH, MEDAGE, and VIOLNTCRIME missing. The second equation has MEDHOME, POPDEN, UNEMP, and PROPCRIME missing. The third equation has MEDHOME, POPDEN, UNEMP, DEATH, and MEDAGE missing. The order condition is therefore satisfied by all equations.

(c) First regress each of POLICE, PROPCRIME, and VIOLNTCRIME against a constant, MEDHOME, POPDEN, UNEMP, DEATH, and MEDAGE, and save the predicted values. In the second stage use these predicted values in place of the actual values and estimate the three equations. In obtaining residuals and standard errors however, actual values will be used. Thus

$$\hat{w} = POLICE - \hat{\gamma}_1 - \hat{\gamma}_2 \, PROPCRIME - \hat{\gamma}_3 \, VIOLNTCRIME$$

EX 13.6

Practice Computer Session 13.2 gives the *ECSLIB* commands for this. The directly estimated reduced form is

$$\hat{Y}_t = 8.282 + 0.139G_t + 2.546T_t + 0.735X_t + 0.949M_t$$
$$\;\;\;\;\;\;\;(0.1)\;\;\;\;\;\;(0.4)\;\;\;\;\;\;\;(6.8)\;\;\;\;\;\;(2.7)\;\;\;\;\;\;\;(9.4)$$

These values are very different from the implied reduced form estimated in Section 13.7. Because the TSLS estimates take account of overidentifying restrictions, they are more efficient than direct OLS estimates of the reduced form. Furthermore, the pairwise correlation coefficients among G_t, T_t, and M_t are all over 0.9. This multicollinearity could account for the unexpected sign for the coefficient T_t.

EX 13.7

We only sketch the steps without going into any details. First copy the file *ps13-2.inp* as *ex13-7.inp*. Then convert all financial variables (except the interest rate) to per capita by dividing them by the population. These variables are then used in exactly the same form. The results are quite similar to those when levels are used instead of per capita.

EX 13.8

Practice Computer Session 13.2 has the *ECSLIB* commands needed to answer this part. OLS estimates of the dynamic model are given below.

$$\hat{C}_t = \underset{(-11.3)}{-235.940} + \underset{(7.3)}{0.735\ DY_t} + \underset{(1.0)}{0.102\ DY_{t-1}}$$

$$\hat{I}_t = \underset{(-3.3)}{-62.778} + \underset{(6.9)}{0.627 DY_t} \underset{(-4.2)}{-0.395 DY_{t-1}} + \underset{(1.8)}{9.036 r_t} - \underset{(-2.9)}{14.817 r_{t-1}}$$

$$\hat{r}_t = \underset{(-0.8)}{-0.907} + \underset{(1.3)}{0.009 Y_t} + \underset{(4.4)}{0.010 Y_{t-1}} + \underset{(-0.2)}{0.00088 M_t} - \underset{(-3.4)}{0.027 M_{t-1}}$$

The corresponding TSLS estimates are as follows:

$$\hat{C}_t = \underset{(-10.8)}{-244.349} + \underset{(6.8)}{0.936\ DY_t} - \underset{(-0.7)}{0.101\ DY_{t-1}}$$

$$\hat{I}_t = \underset{(-3.4)}{-70.917} + \underset{(5.1)}{0.761 DY_t} - \underset{(-3.4)}{0.534 DY_{t-1}} + \underset{(1.9)}{14.667 r_t} - \underset{(-2.7)}{19.420 r_{t-1}}$$

$$\hat{r}_t = \underset{(-0.9)}{-1.071} + \underset{(1.3)}{0.016 Y_t} + \underset{(3.8)}{0.006 Y_{t-1}} \underset{(-0.2)}{-0.00164 M_t} - \underset{(-3.2)}{0.030 M_{t-1}}$$

The implied reduced form equation for GNP is given below.

$$\hat{Y}_t = C_t + I_t + G_t + X_t$$

$$= -244.349 + 0.936\ (\hat{Y}_t - T_t) - 0.101\ (Y_{t-1} - T_{t-1}) - 70.917$$

$$+ 0.761\ (\hat{Y}_t - T_t) - 0.534\ (Y_{t-1} - T_{t-1})$$

$$+ 14.677\ [-1.071 + 0.016\ \hat{Y}_t + 0.006\ Y_{t-1}$$

$$- 0.000164\ M_t - 0.030\ M_{t-1}] - 19.420\ r_{t-1} + G_t + X_t$$

$$= -330.98507 + 1.931832\ \hat{Y}_t - 0.546938\ Y_{t-1} + G_t + X_t$$

$$- 1.697\ T_t + 0.635\ T_{t-1} - 19.420\ r_{t-1}$$

$$- 0.00240702 M_t - 0.44031 M_{t-1}$$

135

Solving for $\hat{Y}_t$ we get the implied form as

$$\hat{Y}_t = 355.198 - 1.073\,G_t + 1.821\,T_t - 1.073\,X_t + 0.00258\,M_t$$
$$+ 0.587\,Y_{t-1} - 0.681\,T_{t-1} + 0.473\,M_{t-1} + 20.841\,r_{t-1}$$

The impact, interim, and long-run multipliers make absolutely no sense. There are three possible reasons for this result; (a) the single period lag may not be enough, more lags might be required, (b) multicollinearity among all the independent variables could have made individual coefficients reverse signs, and (c) serial correlation among residuals may be present.

EX 13.9
Per capita values are obtained in the manner described in Exercise 13.7. The results are similar to those in Exercise 13.8. In particular, multipliers do not make any more sense in this case than in that in Exercise 13.8.

EX 13.10 Standard macro theory states that changes in money supply cause changes in the unemployment and inflation rates. The question here is, "do changes in unemployment and inflation rates affect money supply?". This can be addressed by examining whether unemployment and inflation rates *Granger cause* money supply using equations (13.11) and (13.12). Practice Computer Session 13.3 has the commands needed to answer this question. It is seen that the Wald F-statistic to test the null hypothesis that past unemployment and inflation rates do not affect the current money supply is 1.7996 and the corresponding p-value is 0.013. Thus the null hypothesis is strongly rejected and hence there is support for the notion that money supply is not quite exogenous.